BLIND FAITH

'Lighten our darkness, we beseech Thee, oh Lord.'

BLIND FAITH

as portrayed in the life of William Moon, 1818-1894.
Pioneer in bringing sight to the blind.

by
Edna Stroud

Edna Stroud

William Sessions Limited
York, England

ISBN 1 85072 116 5

© Edna Stroud 1992

Printed in 10 on 11 point Plantin
by William Sessions Ltd
The Ebor Press
York, England

Acknowledgments

To those friends who helped and encouraged me, my sincere thanks.
They each know to whom I refer, also how grateful I am.

Catherine, Deirdre, Elizabeth, Ivy and John, Margery, Mildred, Olive,
Peter and Ron.

Cover design by Phillipa C. Drakeford.

References

Dr Moon And His Work, and various pamphlets... RNIB.

Preface

DURING THE LAST CENTURY, blind William Moon devoted the whole of his manhood to the teaching and care of the blind.

Until he began this great work any blind were completely neglected. He changed all this, visiting them and teaching them to read. In order to achieve this, he invented a method of embossed type and this is still in use today. It is particularly useful to those who lose their reading sight but who are physically unable to distinguish the dots of Braille.

William's work spread across the whole world. His method was used as far away as China.

William Moon's determination, generosity, and above all, his tremendous Christian faith never failed throughout his long life, which lasted from 1818 to 1894. Thousands of blind were helped by him during this time, and he left a legacy of hope which, even today enables the blind to be able to read.

Hitherto, his intimate life has not been portrayed. I have attempted, with some imagination, to paint a picture of what it might well have meant for him.

I now invite you to read on...

Edna Stroud
Hampshire
1990-1992

Chapter 1

THE BEECH TREE SHOOK its head. Its young leaves, already coppery, swayed and shook in the light breeze, as dark, heavy hair might have swayed shaken by the wearer's bent head. It was a magnificent specimen of deep copper beech, and it shaded two gardens to the right and left, from the bright sunlight. Those living in its vicinity were grateful to it, and felt themselves fortunate that, even in a town, such a tree should be living.

Underneath the tree sat a lad in his early teens. He was a thoughtful boy, and one who loved nature. He looked up into the tree top, and ran his hand caressingly down its trunk, appreciating the firmness of the bark and its smooth texture. Such things delighted him, and he let his mind dwell upon the wonders of trees, flowers, and particularly birds. The sound of bird song, the sigh of wind through branches, gave him a deep pleasure.

He was a lanky youth, not yet fully grown but, in spite of his rather gangling limbs, there was a presence about him. Dark haired and with deep brown eyes, he was of a quite striking appearance.

There was a sound. Someone coming out of the back door of the house. There was a movement to his right and his name was called. He turned in the direction of the sound, and it was noticeable that he turned his body almost completely round in order to see who was approaching. He was blind in his right eye.

It was his mother who had called him. She walked towards him and spoke: 'What are you doing? The tea is on the table.'

She was a fairly tall, upright woman, who held herself erect. Her hair, now showing streaks of grey, was covered for the most part, by a dainty, black lace cap. She wore an ankle length skirt of black serge, and a black, lace trimmed blouse, for she was still in mourning. He husband had died several years previously, but the custom was to wear black for some years, probably until the end of life. She wore at her waist a long, white linen apron, and the slight breeze lifted the corner of it. Across her shoulders was a black knitted fichou of fine wool, for although it was not really cold, she felt a slight chill in the air.

In the boy's hand was a slate, on which two or three lines of a poem were written in rather large letters. He had taken to this method of learning anything he needed to know, when he was a small boy in school. He could not see very clearly, even with his left eye, and it was his custom to get other boys to dictate to him what was being learned, so that he might get it by heart. This was to stand him in good stead in later life, as his memory was to be called upon to be his standby. On the slate at present were a few words from Milton's L'Allegro, a poem which gave him great pleasure and satisfaction, even joy. Said his mother, 'You'll take a long time to learn all that, since you cannot get much written on that slate. Let me help you.'

His mother took the slate and noticed, with a pang, that even in the large, white-chalked words, her son had not been able to see to write clearly. 'Let's go in to tea, William,' she said. 'We'll learn this together, and I think we shall have it clearly in our minds before bedtime tonight.' As they walked in, his mother noticed that William stumbled once or twice, and did not appear to see clearly where he was going. She had noticed lately, that he seemed more withdrawn than he had done, and made up her mind that she would have the doctor take another look at her son. She did not comment, but watched him with more than her usual care.

That same evening mother and son sat down with Milton's L'Allegro laid before them. Both William and his mother were deeply sensitive to the poetry of the great man, yet not aware of how much his blindness would mean to them. L'Allegro gave each of them a delight which they shared with each other. When, at bedtime they parted for their own rooms, they each felt an exultation of spirit.

William's mother, having quietly decided that she would get the advice of their doctor about William's eyesight, set about making plans immediately after clearing away their breakfast. She said nothing to her son, but, on the pretext of having to go out for a few necessary provisions, she left him to his studies.

The doctor was an elderly man, and a very kind one. He had, himself, made a mental reservation to talk to William's mother with a view to finding a solution to his problem of decreasing sight. He knew that William was intended for the Ministry, and that he spent many hours in Bible study, both at home and with the help of the local clergyman, and he was impressed by the boy's determination. The doctor was delighted to see his visitor and welcomed her warmly.

'It is good to see you, my dear. And how are you, and William?'

'We're very well, really, doctor, but I am concerned again about William's eyes. Or, I should say, eye. It seems to me that his left eye is failing, and if that happened, there would be no possibility at all of his entering the Ministry.'

After a few minutes of discussion about how William was behaving as regards seeing in general, the doctor decided that he must have a look at the boy, but without raising his suspicions that all might not be well. It was agreed that he should call in on the family, next time he was down their way.

A few days later the doctor was driving his gig towards the cottage where William lived with his mother. As he approached he looked keenly at the neat row of cottages.

They were on the outskirts of the seaside town, and had been built early in the eighteenth century. Some of them were in need of repair, as was the Moon's own cottage, but it was noticeable that theirs was carefully looked after. The windows shone; crisp curtains hung there, and the small garden at the front was a well tended one. The doctor let his thoughts dwell on the occupants. He had known the widow's husband for a short time, and he wondered how she would be able to manage without his support. Money was not plentiful, but she was a proud woman, and a capable one, and he felt sure that she would endure. She was that type... nothing daunted her, and with her son to look after, she was fulfilled in her present situation. Nevertheless, he would never be surprised if she and her son eventually had to move to rooms, rather than have the upkeep of even a small cottage, on her hands. He went up to the door and knocked.

Mrs Moon welcomed the doctor warmly, seating him in the only armchair beside the fireplace in the neat sitting room. The flooring was of red tiles and not entirely even, nor warm, but before the fireplace was a thick, pegged rag rug, and this made a comforting resting place for the feet. Mrs Moon herself had made it and it made a gay addition to the otherwise slightly drab surroundings. It was a homely room.

'William is outside,' she said. 'I'll go and call him.'

'Wait just a moment,' the doctor said. 'I would like to have a chat with you before I see William.'

As they chatted, the doctor glanced around the room. It was simple, but comfortable. The high black fireplace with its shining bars looking welcoming, as did its highly polished fire irons and fender. Although not cold, there was a small fire adding greatly to the comfort of the room.

After a few minutes of general chat, the doctor spoke about William.

'What is the present problem?'

'I am very concerned, doctor,' replied the woman. 'It is my belief that William's sight in his 'good' eye, is deteriorating. He makes very little fuss about it, and, as you know, he is determined to study for the Ministry. I fear that if that became impossible it would go very hard with him.'

'Let me have a general chat. We won't tell him that I came especially to see him, but I will do what I can to find out how his sight is.'

At that moment, William entered the room.

'Oh, good morning, Doctor Hanson. I did not know you were here, but I certainly thought I heard your horse.'

'Yes, you did. I daresay he would be glad of a word with you before we leave. He knows a good friend when he meets one, and does not forget.'

'I will certainly speak to him. Mother, have we an apple or a carrot I can give him?'

'Yes, of course. They're in the basket in the outhouse. Go and get one now, and then come back in.'

William went off to find his present for the horse, and as he stepped over the doorsill outside, they heard him stumble.

'You see, doctor? He is always stumbling about, and it is not like him.'

William went out to give the horse his gift. Animals were special to him, and whenever he met a dog, or any local animal, they seemed to know that William was about.

Back indoors, William seated himself on a stool placed beside the table, and drew towards him a folder containing writing paper. A large copy of the Bible lay beside him.

'I'm anxious to finish my notes on part of Isaiah,' he remarked. 'I won't disturb you both.'

Before he could begin to write, Doctor Hanson spoke.

'And how did Brandy like the fruit? And did you notice the new fittings on his harness?'

'Oh, he took the apple most delicately; he always does, you know. No, I did not see any new fittings.'

The doctor and William's mother exchanged glances. The new fittings were prominent to the eye. Mrs Moon had seen them herself a few days before.

'How are the studies going, William?" asked the doctor.

'Rather slowly I fear. It seems to take me some time to get it all written down, but that does not worry me unduly. I still have a year or two before I need present myself to the Clergy Council.'

'Well, persevere, my boy. I know you are very determined to go into the Ministry. I wish you well.'

With a word of thanks, William opened his Bible and began to write.

Doctor Hanson rose, and William's mother accompanied him to the door. The doctor told her that he had seen what the position was, and that he would keep a watchful eye on William's progress.

'After all,' he said, 'it could right itself. If it does, no one will be more thankful than I. If it does not, well, then, we must see what action we have to take. I'll certainly keep an eye on him.'

As he drove away, Doctor Hanson let his thoughts dwell once again on the occupants of that cottage. His admiration for William's mother grew every time he had contact with her. Left alone, with a son to bring up, limited income, and the heavy responsibility of keeping the house in good repair, William's doubtful health, and the prospect of his sight becoming weaker, yet she kept a brave face, and took charge of every situation as it arose.

William's sister Jane, a little older than her brother, although not always at home, would always help him in any way she could. She spent a few hours once or twice a week helping an elderly lady who lived not too far away, and who needed someone to read to her. It sometimes happened that Jane would stay overnight with her employer, particularly if the old lady should not be well. It was thus that she was not at home during Doctor Hanson's recent call upon her mother and brother.

Jane's opinion of William was a little different from that of their mother. Jane herself felt that William's determination would see him through any difficulty, and in that, William took after his mother whose courage was of the strongest in adversity. But, whereas their mother was of the opinion that should William not be able to complete his study for the Ministry, Jane felt sure that, although he would undoubtedly be bitterly disappointed, he would turn to an alternative of some kind, at the same time thanking the Lord that this was possible. William's faith, Jane knew, was like a rock, and really stronger than one would have expected in so young a boy. When, as a child, William had found it very difficult to follow the lessons at school, he had, even then, done his utmost to learn by heart whatever was required of him, and, in doing so, shown a serenity which was remarkable. She thought she knew her brother better than her mother did. No doubt it was to be expected that a mother would suffer for a deprived child in ways which those nearer in age, and not of so vital a relationship, would not experience. She was very fond of her brother, and determined that she would give him all the support of which she was capable.

II

As time went on, William kept a regular attendance at the clergyman's house, where he was making a thorough study of the Scriptures. At times the going was difficult and much concentration was needed, but William persevered and thoroughly enjoyed the study. As his eighteenth birthday approached, Doctor Hanson suggested that a close and careful look at the boy's eyes might be beneficial.

It was, therefore, convenient that on his way to the clergyman's house one morning, William should meet Doctor Hanson unexpectedly.

'Good morning, sir,' said William.

'Morning, William. What is your errand?'

'I'm due at the Manse in ten minutes for another lesson on Isaiah. I do so enjoy that particular book.'

'Shall we walk on together then?' suggested the doctor. 'I am in no immediate hurry, and am giving the nag a rest today. Like the rest of us, he gets no younger.'

After a few moments, the doctor drew William's attention to a board which had been erected on a nearby wall, containing some message to the community.

'I can't quite make out what that board says, William,' said Doctor Hanson. 'Can you tell me? I think it is to do with a couple of houses that are to be demolished, but I'm not certain.'

Doctor Hanson was taken aback at William's answer. 'Which board?' was the boy's reply.

Anxious not to be alarmist, Doctor Hanson pointed out quietly that the board was placed by the hedgerow at the side of the actual piece of road that they were walking on. Admittedly, it was to William's right, which was always difficult for him on account of the complete blindness of that eye. However, by turning his head he should have been able to see not only the board, but its writing as well. Doctor Hanson was perturbed.

'Never mind it, William,' he said. 'I daresay if it is of any great importance we shall hear about it soon enough. But tell me, are you really unable to see it at all?'

William had to admit that this was so, and the two walked on in silence for a few yards. They were nearing the Manse, and the doctor suggested to William that he might look in at his surgery when he had finished the lesson. William agreed to this, and turned in at the gate of the Manse. In his secret heart he was anxious, as it was becoming more apparent that his eyesight was not as good as it had been a couple of months before. He knew that Doctor Hanson had his welfare at heart, and he knew why. He tried not to face it too often.

Doctor Hanson poured himself a glass of madeira and sat, deep in thought, in the armchair. He was becoming more and more concerned about William and his prospects. The boy was of an unusual seriousness and his evangelical up-bringing was having its effect. Doctor Hanson knew that it was William's habit to pray about any problem which he met with, and that he had, in spite of increasing difficulties, a sublimity of spirit unusual in one so young. This, the doctor thought, was likely to stand the boy in good stead.

The doorbell rang, and the doctor, expecting that it was William at the door, answered it himself.

'Come in, William,' he said warmly, and led him to the surgery.

'And how did the lesson go, this morning?' asked the doctor.

'Very well, I'm glad to say,' said William. 'I find it most rewarding and very satisfying, studying the Scriptures with the Minister. I would like to feel that when I come to the preaching eventually, I might do it as well as our Minister does.'

'What will be your next step, then?' asked Doctor Hanson.

'I am to apply for admission to the training school,' answered William. 'All being well, I shall be starting my final training at the beginning of next year.'

Doctor Hanson was at a loss as to how to continue the conversation on a cheerful note, but he knew that in all fairness to William, he must pursue what he felt necessary.

'William,' he said, 'I have to admit that I am very concerned about the state of your eyesight, and so is your mother. Have you found any difficulty in the reading you have to do?'

William hesitated. Eventually he said, 'Sometimes, I have to admit, I have to stop studying in order to rest my eyes.'

The word 'eyes' was significant as William tried to see things in the normal manner, and to forget that he was already completely blind in his right eye. Although as a young boy, he had had to ask help from his schoolmates in order to be able to follow the lessons, he tried to behave as his friends did, and tried to put his difficulties behind him.

Doctor Hanson took a turn about the room, and then came to stand beside William. He spoke gently.

'My boy, I feel that it might be as well if we tried to have a more experienced man have a closer look at your 'good' eye. If you could agree to this, I could take you to see a friend of mine who is an expert in such matters. What do you say?'

William did not answer at once. He sat in silence, and the thought came into his mind that his future as a minister of religion might be jeopardised. As indeed, it very well might if his sight really failed. Such a thought was anathema to him, but with his usual attitude of faith, he answered Doctor Hanson quietly.

'I realise that you, as well as my mother, are concerned for me, and I have to admit to you, Doctor Hanson, that I find reading a strain, very often. If you think there might be benefit to be obtained, I will do as you wish. The Ministry means everything to me, as I think you know, and I believe that

Mother is anxious that I should achieve my ambition if at all possible.'

'Well done, William,' said the doctor. 'I will arrange a visit to the eye specialist, and will let you know what can be done, as soon as I have contacted him.'

William left the doctor's house in two minds. He did not want to admit that he had any disability, but, on the other hand, if there were any danger of his not continuing with his studies, he must know.

William's birthday fell in December, and it was after this event that he heard again from Doctor Hanson. As it was nearly Christmas, the appointment was made for the visit to the specialist in the new year. It would be an eventful year in any case, as it was during that time that the new young Queen Victoria acceded to the throne of England.

It was not until February that Doctor Hanson was able to take William to the important appointment. They had about ten miles to travel, and Doctor Hanson called for William in his gig. William's mother was not a little alarmed at the thought of possible expense, but the good doctor reassured her.

'I want to do this for you and William,' he told her. 'I have a great regard for you both, and feel that whatever I am able to do to help William, will be a reward in itself. At least, we shall have tried.'

Bowling along out of the town, and over the coast road, gave William a sense of well being. The countryside had been frozen, but was beginning to thaw and to show some fresh green. There were snowdrops in the hedgerows, and a sense of expectation in the air.

The specialist proved to be a very kindly man, who received William with special interest, and Doctor Hanson as an old friend. They were taken in and given a warming toddy, chatting the while. The eye specialist paid particular attention to William's behaviour as regards his seeing about him. Presently, Doctor White, the specialist, suggested that they retire to his surgery and begin their explorations.

Doctor White was extremely thorough, and it was not until an hour later that he sat down again before his desk, and talked seriously to his visitors.

'Now, William,' he said, 'I must be quite frank with you. I feel sure that you would prefer a plain, direct statement from me, than to be at the receiving end of a lot of ineffectual chat.'

William agreed, and Doctor Hanson also seemed satisfied. He knew, and was sure that by now the specialist had decided, that William was a strong character and well able to make right decisions of whatever nature they might be.

Doctor White then said... 'I fear, William, that the sight of your eye is not likely to respond to any treatment that I can offer. I think it would be advisable for you to come to terms with the situation immediately. We will do all that we can to help you, but it seems to me that your sight is fading fast.'

William sat still. He turned from one doctor to the other, and then said, 'And what about the Ministry?'

Doctor Hanson had explained in some detail to Doctor White what William's ambition was, and that he was studying ready for admission to the training college for preparation to be a minister of religion.

For a while they all sat silent, and then William said, 'God will not fail me. I intend to continue studying the Scriptures, and it will then be made clear to me what my next steps must be. I thank you most sincerely for your kindness and care.'

Doctor White laid a hand on the boy's shoulder. 'Well done, William. I admire your courage, and I shall be most interested to learn how you go on.'

They then left the doctor's house, and drove back home.

William's mother was at the door to meet them. Her face expressed her anticipation of possible help for William.

His mother kissed William and shook hands warmly with Doctor Hanson. They then went inside and sat down before a cheerful fire. The doctor passed a searching glance towards Mrs Moon and, as their eyes met, he very slightly shook his head.

William broke the silence. 'I enjoyed my visit to Doctor White, Mother,' he said. 'He was most kind to me, and took great pains. I might as well tell you at once that he holds out no great hope of my sight improving. Nevertheless, I shall continue my studies and await events.'

Mrs Moon smiled gently. 'Very well, son,' she said. 'You will get all the support we can give you, as you know.'

Doctor Hanson then rose, and said he must be away at once.

'The nag will need a rub down, and I have to prepare to see a couple of patients later this evening.'

After he had gone, William took out his books again, and sat at the table bending low over them. His mother sighed. She was afraid for him.

III

1837 passed, with all the excitement of the new Queen. How young she was. Many shook their heads over the responsibility she had taken upon herself, but, as time wore on, they became accustomed to the situation. The next year was one of further trial for William.

William's mother and sister went out of their way to help him in his studies, reading passages to him, and sometimes copying out passages which he wanted particularly to refer to. The year wore on, and William decided that he must put in his application for his study course before he was twenty. The Minister who was conducting William's study at home, had occasion to visit Mrs Moon one day when William and his sister had gone for a walk.

After exchanging greetings, Mrs Moon asked the Minister for his candid opinion upon William's progress and prospects.

'He will be twenty in December, won't he?' said the Minister.

'That is right. He was anxious to have a place in the college by then,' replied Mrs Moon.

'I am afraid that there will be great disappointment for him,' went on the Minister. 'I have watched him most carefully, and I see more times than I care to tell you, that he is quite at a loss. He can scarcely see what he is doing. A place in college in his condition is out of the question. What are we to do?'

Mrs Moon sat thoughtfully silent. 'He must be told, of course,' she said. 'I cannot let him go into his twenty-first year still under the impression that all will be well. How shall we break it to him?'

The Minister considered for some moments. Then he said:

'Prayer is certainly called for, and great patience. If William cannot become a minister of religion, what WILL he do? We must deal with him gently.'

William and his sister were heard coming up the pathway. The two friends were silent and apprehensive of what should be said.

William then came into the room, his sister having gone to take off her walking shoes. The young man spoke to his mother, but ignored the Minister.

'William,' said his mother. 'Do you not see that the Minister is here?'

'I'm sorry, Mother. No, I did not see him. Good afternoon, sir,' he said, and turned in the opposite direction from that in which the Minister sat. Gently, his mother took his arm. 'Come,' she said. 'Let us all sit down together. Jane will bring us tea, I'm sure.'

William was then able to shake the Minister's hand and at that moment his sister entered with a tray.

'Good afternoon, Minister,' she said. 'I saw you through the window as we came up the path, and I decided that a cup of tea would be the right reception for you. I will pour it.'

Jane dispensed tea, placing a cup for William on the table by which he was sitting. She then addressed the Minister...

'It is good to see you, Minister. Perhaps you have news of William's admission to the college?'

Mrs Moon was perturbed. This was a more direct approach to their present problem than she had anticipated. She did not speak, however, but waited to hear what the Minister would reply.

'I am afraid, William,' he said, addressing William directly, 'that it is not good news at all. This is why I came over this afternoon to discuss the matter with you and your mother.'

'I feel,' said William quickly, 'that we would do better to face the situation at once, and find out what I must do to continue my studies.'

'In that case,' said the Minister, 'I must tell you at once that there is no possibility of your being allowed to enter the college. I am bitterly sorry for you, as I know how much you desire to join the ministry. However, there is no prospect for you in that profession as they could not consider taking on a near blind person. Believe me, William, I am truly sorry.'

Mrs Moon gripped the arms of her chair and looked intently towards William to see what the effect of the Minister's words might be. William said nothing. He stood up and walked about the room. It was noticeable how Jane watched him carefully, and took hold of the teapot in case William should knock it over. He knew his way about his home, but in an anxious moment such as the present one, when he was not paying particular attention to his movements, anything could happen. Presently William spoke again.

'I am not blind yet. Not completely. I can still see about me a little.'

His mother said, 'Dear William, try not to be too disheartened. We have the doctors' opinions, and there seems to be little hope that you can enter the ministry. We will all help you...'

William then fled the room. They saw him in the garden, leaning his head against his adored beech tree. Mrs Moon remarked that they had better leave him alone at the moment.

'He will find his own salvation,' she said to the Minister and Jane. 'It is very hard for him, but we must take into account his great faith, and his determination to be of service in the world.'

The Minister raised his right hand as if in blessing. 'His faith, my dear Mrs Moon, is remarkable in one so young. He is more mature in that respect than many a minister I could name. We must pray for him, and keep a constant watch for his welfare.'

He then got up to leave them, and when William returned, his mother and Jane were sitting alone, their concern apparent in their faces.

William's dream of becoming a minister of religion was not to be fulfilled. By the early spring of eighteen forty, his sight had left him. He was completely blind.

In spite of William's strength of character, and his firm belief in God, he found the next few weeks almost unbearable.

If he was not to be able to enter the ministry, what then was there for him to do? At last there came a day when he felt that his life was useless. That particular day had been long and depressing. That morning a friend of his mother's had called upon them and talked for some time about William's condition and his prospects. What were his prospects, anyway, was the thought uppermost in William's troubled mind.

It was September, and the nights were beginning to draw in. As darkness fell, William found himself wandering about the house in an unsettled mood. Eventually, he unbolted the back door and felt his way into the darkening garden.

There was a light breeze which ruffled the leaves of his beloved beech tree. Although there was fitful moonlight, this was of no consequence to William. Blindness had claimed him. His mother, William thought, was perhaps too optimistic about the possibilities of a useful future for her son. He felt, indeed, in spite of his faith, that his life lay in ruins. What was to become of him? All these years during his late teens and now his early twenties, he had cherished his ambition and worked exceedingly hard in order to achieve it. He drew near to the beech tree, and sank down upon the bench beneath it. How often had he come here to think, even to pray? He prayed now, even in his deep despair, asking God what use could possibly be made of his dark life? If he was not to be a minister or religion, what else was there for him to do?

It was said that everything was for the best under God's guidance. But how could that be so when he was so inflicted with helplessness?

So deep was his despair then, that William dropped his head in his hands and, although feeling not a little ashamed to be using the words which Christ Himself had used, he prayed with intense feeling... 'Father, if it be Thy will, let this cup pass from me.' Tears sprang unbidden to his blind eyes. 'Dear God, help me,' he prayed.

After a time he felt calmer. He knew that, at all costs, he must keep his faith which meant everything to him. As he felt calmer, he rose from the bench, passed his hands caressingly across the smooth trunk of the tree, and began to make his careful way back into the house.

As he bolted the back door he heard his mother call him. He knew that, although she had retired to bed, she would have known that he had been outside, and was waiting anxiously for his return.

'Is anything amiss, William?' she called.

'No, Mother. I have been outside to get a little air. I will come up now.'

William felt his way upstairs and into his room. As soon as he reached its privacy, he fell upon his knees beside his bed. Covering his face with both hands, he knelt silently for a few moments. Then he prayed for strength to accept whatever lay in store for him.

'Whatever Thou wilt, I will do.'

Then, lying quite quietly he finally fell asleep.

Chapter 2

NEWS OF THE PLIGHT of Mrs Moon's son gradually became known in the neighbourhood. William made no fuss, but it was plain that he could scarcely hide his deep disappointment at not being able to achieve his ambition. Who could blame a young man in the prime of life, no matter how strong-minded, for sometimes finding it almost unbearable to be so helpless. When the sun shone, he would spend long hours in the garden, sitting under the beech tree. He would then rehearse to himself favourite passages from the Scriptures. His mother and sister helped him as much as they could, by reading to him, either from the Bible, or poetry, of which he was inordinately fond.

William attended the non-conformist church with his mother, and with Jane when she was at home, and their friends among the congregation were exceedingly kind. It was, no doubt, through contacts with them that an unexpected happening occurred.

One day there was a knock at the door. Mrs Moon went to answer it and found an unknown lady standing there.

'I think I have come to the right house,' said the visitor. 'I am looking for William Moon.'

'Oh yes, William lives here. I am his mother.'

'I have come with a suggestion which I would wish to put to you and William, particularly to William. Is he home?'

'Oh yes. Do come in.' Mrs Moon led the way to the sitting room where William was sitting, rather languidly, in his chair by the window.

'William,' said his mother. 'Here is a lady who has come with a suggestion which she wishes to put to you.'

William stood up and shook hands with the visitor...

'I have come,' said the lady, 'because I think I can help you to read again.'

William was astonished. 'By what means,' he wanted to know.

'I have access to a special raised type which has been recently invented by a Mr Frere, and which can be read by hand.'

There was a short silence. Then William asked what this signified and how it could be applied to him.

'If you are willing, I will arrange for you to come to my house two or three times a week to begin with, and I will see that you learn this new method.'

Mrs Moon and William were both overjoyed. Mrs Moon wanted to know what arrangements would have to be made, and how, and when? Could William start at once?

William was as keen as his mother, and his manner showed the excitement which this new proposal had wrought in him.

'I am exceedingly grateful to you,' he told the visitor. 'The prospect of being able at least to make use of my time, is one I cannot ignore. When would it be convenient for us to start this venture?'

Arrangements were therefore made, and William, the very next day, was taken to the home of the lady whom he had previously never met.

The prospect with its possibilities filled William with joyful hope.

As William progressed with learning the new system, he found that there were several other methods of reading from raised type. These he also studied until, after a few months, he was conversant with them all. It was then that his great plan came to his mind.

'Mother,' he said one day, entering the house with an excited expression that she had not seen on his face for some months, 'I am going to find as many blind children as I can, and teach THEM to read.'

'Why, William, that is a splendid idea and one which I feel is worthy of your strength of will.'

'Don't let us boast, Mother. I shall only do anything in the strength of the Lord. But this plan excited me, and I cannot wait to put it into action.'

William set about his task with a will. He searched for, and found, several blind children. Some even deaf and dumb as well. He arranged to bring them all together in his home and, with his mother's co-operation, his small school was launched.

II

William's twenty-second birthday in the December of that year was a much more cheerful occasion than had been anticipated. The past three months had seen an intensity of study which did a great deal for his morale. When his sight had finally failed he had envisaged a long and miserable existence of complete boredom and uselessness. His spirits rose with his learning of the embossed types of reading, and it was apparent to all who knew him that he now had a purpose in life.

He would make the teaching of the blind his life's work, and, with the strength he gained from his prayers and attending his church, his personality began to glow with an inner light.

William's mother was happier than she had ever thought to be again since the death of her husband and the onset of William's blindness. There was now a sense of purpose in all that they did, and the house became happy once more.

William spent many hours visiting the homes of the blind children, and when at last they were able to meet in his own home, William began to feel that something was being achieved. His moments of grave doubt and depression were now rare, and he went about the house singing. Life was becoming good again.

After some time William found that there were more children needing his help than could be accommodated in his mother's house. It was decided that they should approach the Minister of their local chapel, and find out whether he could perhaps offer them the use of, at least, a part of his roomy Sunday School building.

The Minister was delighted to be of assistance to William, and when William called upon him to make his request, he took him inside and made him warmly welcome.

'Come in, my dear boy,' said the Minister, and settled William comfortably before a cheerful fire, pouring him a drink of home made elderberry wine. 'What can I do for you?'

When William told him what he needed, the Minister was thoughtful.

'I will most certainly let you use some space in my school room, William, but first I must speak to my elders. I feel sure they will be agreeable, but you will understand that the proposition you put to me will have to be formal.'

This was understandable and William agreed happily.

'There must also be a body of management of some kind if a school was to be run on satisfactory lines. No doubt there could also be a monetary consideration to be met.'

After some further discussion the Minister agreed that he would contact his church committee at once, and let William know the result of their considerations.

'But have no fear, William,' he concluded. 'I am in favour of the enterprise and wish to help you in any and every way I can. I am so happy that you are finding a vocation in this way, and we are all delighted that you are able to be of such great service.'

A few days after their meeting, the Minister called at the Moon home, and gave William the assurance he sought, that all would be well and that he could now begin to arrange for his blind pupils to meet on a regular basis.

A committee was formed and the official business soon settled. William was happy.

One day, after the school had been functional for some time, William said to his mother, 'I am not satisfied. Some of these methods of reading seem very difficult to me. Many of the children are not able to grasp what is required.'

'So what do you propose then, William?'

'That I do not know as yet, but I shall give it deep thought and prayer.'

At about this time, William attended a function at the local church, where he met a number of interesting people. Not the least of these was a girl of about his own age. William and she found themselves seated together and she was most helpful to him in describing what was going on, who was speaking, and, when it come to taking refreshment at the end of the evening, she helped him with his supper. William was impressed and when he was settling down in his room for the night, she was uppermost in his thoughts.

'I wonder what she looks like?' thought William. He knew that she had a firm handclasp, and a very kindly voice, an attractive one, too. He hoped that they might meet again, and settled down to sleep with the thought that he would be very happy if they did.

Now that William had adequate premises for his class, he went ahead and would have enjoyed the teaching greatly, if he had felt satisfied that all the children understood the lessons. When his kind benefactor had taught him to read from the raised methods, she had also collected together several children, not only blind, but deaf and dumb as well. This made William's task much more difficult, owing to the fact that much time had to be spent in trying to make contact with those heavily handicapped.

One day, as William was walking carefully home at mid-day, deep in thought about how to cope with his pupils to their best advantage, he collided with a person coming from the opposite direction. To his amazed delight, it turned out to be none other than the attractive girl he had met at the evening meeting a week or two before. As soon as she spoke, he knew it was she, and he held out his hand to greet her.

'I do apologise for walking into you,' he said, taking her hand and feeling a little reluctant to let it go again. 'I do try to be most careful, and know the way very well. I must have been dreaming.'

'Please, do not apologise,' replied the girl. 'I, too, was thinking of other things, and had not noticed that you were coming towards me. It is a great pleasure to meet you again.'

'Tell me your name please,' said William. 'We were not introduced the other evening, and I do feel I should know who it was who was so very kind to me.'

'I'm Maria,' replied the girl, 'and I know you are William. Shall we walk together a little way? I can easily turn back with you, as I am not due home to lunch for almost an hour.'

'I should be delighted,' said William. 'I do have to be home quite soon, as I have to return by two o'clock for the next lesson.'

'I heard that you had started a school for blind children in the Sunday School room of the Chapel down the road. I must say, I admire your courage. How are you progressing?'

William offered his arm to his companion, and they walked slowly along. He told her that he had been able to find a number of blind children, and some not so young blind people as well, and that he was doing his best to teach them to read.

'This must be a very difficult task, William,' she said. 'What are you able to teach them?'

'There are various methods of reading by raised type, and I am endeavouring to get them to understand, and to use them. It is not easy, but I feel that this is a task which has been given to me by Providence, and I am happy to do it.'

They were nearing William's home by this time, and Maria said that although she would prefer to stay and talk more to William, she had best turn back home.

'Thank you for walking with me so far,' said William. 'I hope we shall soon meet again.'

'I hope so too, William,' said she sincerely. 'I will come to your school tomorrow, if you will allow me, and walk back home with you.'

William was delighted. 'I look forward to that,' he replied; and they separated. William went in to his mid-day meal in much better spirits than when he had left his schoolroom an hour before.

Mrs Moon greeted her son. 'You're looking remarkably cheerful, William. Has the school gone well this morning?'

William seated himself at the table, and his mother had put before him a dish of mutton stew, before he answered her.

'The school goes quite well, on the whole, Mother. But there are problems, as you will allow, when one tries to teach blind people with no previous knowledge of reading. But yes, I do feel cheered.'

He went on to tell his mother about meeting Maria on his way home, and how she had helped him along. 'She says she will be able to meet me tomorrow, and walk back with me. This would be a great help.'

Mrs Moon considered her son. He certainly did appear happier than of late. She said, 'And who is Maria?'

'She is the daughter of Doctor Black, Mother. I met her at the church two or three weeks ago. I think I told you about it.'

Mrs Moon was not sure. She had no recollection of having heard of the girl. She felt a pang in her heart. She wondered what might happen if William fell in love. He had a very great handicap in his blindness, and, added to this, he was not by any stretch of the imagination, in a position to provide much in the way of finances. She let her thoughts run on for a few moments. No doubt she was imagining things, and putting too great a meaning into what William had said.

William had noticed her silence, and the thought was in his head that perhaps his mother was rather exaggerating, and imagining things which had not, nor very probably ever would, occur. When the time came for him to return for the afternoon session he kissed his mother, and went off, cheerfully enough, on his careful way back to the Sunday School room.

This state of affairs continued for some time. Quite often, Maria Black would meet William as he left the schoolroom, and guide him back home. Naturally enough, they became firm friends.

One day, as they were walking along together, Maria said, 'I would like to come and help you sometimes, in your school, if you think there might be anything useful in such an arrangement.'

William was delighted at the thought, but presently he said, 'Would there be any objection from your parents if you did so?'

'I do not think so,' replied Maria. 'I have no mother, and my father is so busy with his hospital work, that he is hardly ever at home during the day. I am a free agent in my movements as a rule. But I would be quite happy for you to seek the advice of your committee if you thought it right.'

William agreed to her suggestion, but in his heart of hearts he had other ideas.

Maria's suggestion was not put before the committee at once. One day, William asked Maria to come home with him, and to meet his mother and sister. He chose one hot Saturday afternoon when his week's work at the school was finished. Maria seemed happy at the prospect, and she walked over to William's house alone. William had confided in his mother that he was becoming attached to Maria.

Mrs Moon knew her son well enough to know that any ideas that might be stirring in his mind would be prayerfully considered by him, and that there would be no use in trying to deter him from anything he had put his mind to. She acknowledged to herself that it looked as if her original fears, if fears they were, were coming true. She had considerable misgivings nevertheless, for she felt that if William were to be in love, he might be heading for a deep disappointment. However, she agreed to Maria's visit, and looked forward to it with pleasure, as well as some anxiety.

The August Saturday dawned, and William was in a fever of anticipation. There was no doubt at all that he was, by now, in love with Maria. As was his wont, he prayed about the situation regularly in his nightly devotions, and felt that the Lord would guide him aright.

Maria arrived, and they all went outside into the garden to sit under the shade of the great beech tree. Jane went indoors and presently returned with a tray laid with the delicate china which was one of Mrs Moon's earlier treasures. Tea was poured, and William's mother studied her visitor with a keen interest. She was certainly a very pleasant girl, and serious, and, when she looked at William, there was a gentle, caring expression in Maria's face.

When Maria was ready to leave, William said he would escort her back home. Although only of an hour's duration, he was content with the visit and with the reception that Maria had received from his family. He did not at that time enter Maria's own house, but as soon as he had arrived back at his own home he went in search of his mother.

'Well, Mother,' he began. 'Is she not a sweet natured girl?'

'She appears to be,' replied his mother. 'I look forward to seeing her again, and no doubt we shall become very friendly together.'

'I intend to ask her to marry me,' said William.

Mrs Moon did not at once reply. Her fears arose in her heart again. Who would be willing to marry a blind man? And what was her father likely to think of such a plan? But she could do nothing to dissuade her son from his intention, and, in church the next morning she laid the matter, as William always did, before the Lord.

III

When William left his school at mid-day the following day, Maria was there to meet him. This had become a regular habit, and one which William appreciated. Although he always felt his way most carefully when out in the streets, it was comforting to have a companion who could see any unexpected disaster approaching.

Before they had gone many yards, William spoke, and his tone was gently persuasive.

'Maria, I have that to ask you which might be better spoken at home, but I can wait no longer. I want you to marry me.'

Maria was silent, but the pressure of her fingers upon his arm became firmer.

'Oh, William, that would make me very happy. I would gladly accept the responsibility of being able to help you in every way.'

'Maria, you make me a very proud man. I must come to see your father at my first opportunity. When is he likely to be at home, would you think?'

It so happened that Doctor Black was to be at home for a couple of days, prior to his travelling abroad on a medical mission. It seemed that the time was now ripe for William to approach him. He asked Maria to find out from her father when William might call.

Almost at once an appointment was made, and, the next day after the afternoon session of the school, Maria met William and took him home to meet her father.

Doctor Black talked to William about his ambitions and asked him to describe the blind school which he was running. He had to admit that he was impressed by William's firm determination and not a little by his serenity. William left the house of his future father-in-law with a feeling of deep satisfaction. He and Maria would make plans as soon as possible.

A week or two later Doctor Black returned from his Continental visit. He was not in the best of moods, and Maria was disturbed by her father's strange manner.

'What is it, Father?' she asked. 'You seem to be quite upset about something.'

'I have had time to reflect whilst I have been away, and I find, daughter, that I am no longer agreeable to your marrying a blind man. What can he do to earn a reasonable living? Will he be able to support you in any degree of comfort?'

Maria was nonplussed. 'But you said, Father, that you were very agreeable to our marrying.'

'I think my mind was rather pre-occupied with my visit abroad. But now it is quite made up. I cannot support this idea of your marrying a pretty well penniless man who is, what is much worse, a blind man. You will have to cancel your arrangements.'

Maria turned and left the room hurriedly. Tears were not far from her eyes, and she had difficulty in gulping them down. She must see William at once. One thing was quite clear... she would marry William come what may. She loved him, and, since she was always left so much to her own devices at home, she would feel no compunction in leaving it. Her father seemed absorbed in his medical work, and his daughter seemed to be unimportant to him.

William's reaction to Maria's unpleasant news was to take immediate action.

'If your father withdraws his consent, then we must marry without it,' he told Maria. He took her in his arms and told her that together they would face whatever came.

William's mother was not informed of the present state of affairs; they could see no good purpose being served in upsetting her. She had become attached to her future daughter-in-law, and was looking forward to the time when they would be all one family.

Maria did not speak to her father on the subject again. He was, as ever, wrapped up in his work, so she felt quite justified in carrying on with her own plans.

William prayed urgently about his prospects, asking God to help him make a good home for Maria. As always, he felt at peace after his prayers. He looked with eager anticipation towards that day when Maria should be his wife. His great regret was that he could not see this lovely girl with whom he was to spend the rest of his married life. His mother and sister had described her to him, but even so, just to see her, if only for one glimpse so that he could retain the memory, would have been a wonderful gift. They must marry as soon as their plans could be finalised.

As the Autumn drew to a close, nights having drawn in and Winter approaching, they were married. It was November, and William joked that even if he could see, it would be too dark!

The day began with a fog, a sea mist coming up over the town, but by mid-day the air cleared. There was actually a gleam of sunshine as the newly married pair emerged from the chapel. Mrs Moon and Jane hurried on ahead, leaving William and Maria, now also Mrs Moon, to walk at their leisure back home to William's house. The clergyman went along a short time later, and soon they were all sitting comfortably before a welcoming fire, drinking tea.

It had been a very quiet wedding. There was no money for any sort of display. William's mother was in no position to be even slightly extravagant; she had rent to pay for the cottage, and, although the landlord was a reasonable man, she took it upon herself to do as much to the upkeep of her home as she possibly could. Maria's father had cut her off, refusing to contribute in any degree to the upkeep of William's marital home. However, not withstanding all these conditions, it was a very happy little party. It finally broke up, and Jane and her mother stood at the door to say goodbye to William and Maria, bidding them Godspeed as they set off to walk to the home which they had taken in the town. The clergyman gave his blessing, and left.

Mrs Moon and her daughter sat in a contented silence before the fire, thinking with great tenderness of the two young people who had just started out in life together under such difficult circumstances.

'God bless them both,' murmured Mrs Moon. And she and Jane began to put away the tea things, and clear up for the night.

William and Maria walked silently. Maria's arm was tightly linked with her husband's, and his hand closed firmly over hers. The walk was not a long one, and within the hour they were within their new abode. As William remarked, it was only rented accommodation, but at least, they were there together. 'But God,' he prayed silently, 'if I could but just see her.' He tightened his arm about his wife, drew her into their bedroom and gently closed the door.

Chapter 3

WILLIAM AND MARIA WERE SUBLIMELY happy together. William was very contented to know that his wife was near at hand. Although he could not see her, he used to try to visualise her actions as she went about the house. He would listen for her voice and, when he had located her, he would put his arms around her, telling her what a joy it was to have her there. Maria loved him dearly.

It was very fortunate that they were so contented in each other's company, for it was not long before they found themselves in financial straits. What small amount of capital which had been left to him by his father, William soon found to be almost gone. His salary from the school was small, and it was to be even smaller before the Winter was over.

One evening, as they sat resting after supper, Maria said she thought they should try to open a little shop, which would augment their meagre resources. After some discussion, it was decided that this might be a sensible action to take, and, as Maria pointed out, they could open a shop which would give her scope for her expertise in embroidery.

'I feel,' said Maria, 'that there would be a good market for fine linen and embroidery silks. Embroidery is a popular pastime now, and it is a subject about which I know a considerable amount.'

It was then decided that they would make the attempt, and a small shop in the more elegant part of the town was opened.

Alas for their hopes. Although it was nearing Christmas, and Maria had fondly imagined that ladies would be eager to take advantage of such a shop, the venture failed. The rent of the shop, added to the quarterly rent of their house, was a burden which they could not meet. After Christmas, which they spent with William's mother and sister, they were faced with even greater difficulties. Early in the year the weather began to harden. The skies were brilliantly clear at night, and very hard frosts claimed the earth. It became bitterly cold, and snow began to fall and lie on the ground, freezing.

Walking along the streets became very treacherous, and William had to go exceedingly carefully to and from school.

But worse still... his blind pupils were unable to attend the school in any but the very smallest numbers. Sometimes the average attendance fell as low as five each day, and William received a great shock when one day the treasurer of the school committee came to him with a grave face, telling him that as the attendance was so low, finances were even lower, and that he could pay William no more than five shillings a week under the present circumstances.

William's faith was put to a severe test. He went home to tell Maria his grave news.

'How can we manage to pay our way, then?' asked Maria.

'My love, I fear we are going to find it extremely difficult. Our meagre capital is now gone. The shop has not fulfilled our expectations, and we have to find our quarter's rent for this house.'

The next few weeks found the young Moons in real distress. It was not until the weather eased and a feeling of Spring began to fill the air, that William's salary was raised to seven and sixpence a week. But to try to live and meet their expenses was still well nigh impossible. They approached their landlord with a request that he release them from their twelve month agreement, but he would not hear of it. He was adamant! They had signed a contract for one year, and they must honour it.

They let off half the house, hopefully anticipating that by this means they would be able to meet the remainder of the year's rent. Again they were let down. At the end of the quarter when they asked their tenant to pay the due proportion, it was found that the tenant was bankrupt, and had no money to pay them.

'We must leave this house, William,' said Maria. 'We cannot possibly afford to continue to find our quarterly rent.'

William agreed, and they decided to find other accommodation at a cheaper rate. They moved in, and were prepared to let as many rooms as possible and, by this means earn enough money to pay the new rent, and to pay off their account with their former landlord. Misfortune dogged them. It was yet another three months before they made the first letting. Even William, usually so confident, began to despair. All seemed so dark to them both.

Eventually they were driven to approach their new landlord, to ask if he would release them but he, with the same brusque manner as the first one, refused to meet them in this way.

The young Moons were indeed now reduced to a state of want. There were days when they had difficulty in finding enough food. Often they would go a whole day on one very small meal. William's seven shillings and sixpence a week was as a drop in the ocean of their needs.

The warmer weather made matters a little easier, but life was a severe strain. They did receive some help from sympathetic friends and William's mother, but Maria was particularly affected by the straits in which they found themselves, for she was by now pregnant.

When eventually, Maria confided to William that she was expecting their first child, he was overjoyed, but when he began to consider their position, their lack of money, and the difficulties which they were facing, he was gravely concerned. Then, in his usual manner, he prayed long and earnestly for help and guidance.

'I feel,' he told Maria, 'that it can be only a blessing that we should have a child. I hope you feel so as well.'

Maria did her best in her usual patient manner, and tried not to worry about how they were to make ends meet. She had, after all, been, as William himself also had, well over two months with no regular meals. She began to doubt their action in taking on the second house, but, after all, she told herself, William had thought it the right thing to do. She must be careful to keep her thoughts constructive, or she felt she might begin to doubt William herself. What WERE they to do?

The rent of their first house was twenty pounds a year, and this had to be settled every quarter, but where were they to find enough money? The rent from the letting of the rooms in their second house must be used, and this was little enough in all conscience. Then they must pay their new rent as well.

Maria's thoughts went round in bewildering circles, and there were times when she felt almost deranged as a consequence. How they managed to live through the rest of that year she would never know, but live they did, and early in the next year their son was born.

William found himself holding in his arms the smallest human being he had ever encountered. He could feel hands, with tiny fingers; feet with even tinier toes, and hair which Maria told him was dark like his own, lying like silk beneath his gentle touch. There was but one thing which William found hard to endure. He could not see this miracle which had happened to them. He knelt beside the bed, after handing back his son to Maria's eager hands, and she held William's hand in a firm grip, fully realising what he must be enduring.

II

When the baby was a few weeks old, the Moons heard rumours of a great surgeon in London who was doing miraculous things with people's eyes.

Their surprise was very great, when a friend came to them and suggested that they might go up to see if any help would be possible for William.

'This would be far beyond us,' answered William. 'We could not possibly find such an amount of money.'

'My friend,' replied his visitor, 'I should feel it a great privilege to finance such a venture. Your work with those blind children is worthy of every support which can be given. Please, I beg, allow me to do this for you.'

William and Maria were overcome.

The next few days were exciting and busy ones for the Moons. It was their first venture together, and the mere prospect of a train journey was alarming. William's mother suggested that she might have care of the child whilst they were away, but that, said Maria, although very kind, was out of the question since she must continue to feed him herself. At last, the day came, and they set off eagerly for the little station.

The train, although not necessarily a Parliamentary one, took its time to get from Brighton to Battersea where the London terminus then was. The seats were hard, and Maria found difficulty in getting comfortable with the baby in her arms. But all this was of secondary importance to them both. Their hopes were high, and, as Maria said, only suppose that the great surgeon were able to help William, what a difference it would make to their lives. William was his usual quiet, confident self, however, and warned Maria not to set her hopes too high.

Arriving in London they found the lodging which had been booked for the week. It was clean and comfortable, and they made themselves at home there, eating a sustaining cooked supper with relish.

The next day William kept his appointment at the hospital. A tall and rather dignified nurse, her ankle length uniform swishing about her as she walked, took charge of William, and finally ushered him in to the august presence.

The surgeon asked William many questions. He looked long and hard into both William's eyes, and eventually at the end of an hour's talk and examination, suggested that William might come into the hospital for a couple of days, so that a closer inspection could be made. This William agreed to, and, after he had made sure that their landlady would have special care of his wife and baby whilst he was away, he knelt in prayer beside his bed, and committed himself and his actions to the Lord, requesting Him to keep Maria safe.

They both went to the hospital the next morning, and, after seeing him installed, and having the nurse's reassurance that William would be in excellent hands, she went back to the lodging to await events.

On the second day of his stay in the hospital, the surgeon made a deep and careful, and rather painful, inspection of William's eyes again. As there were no anaesthetics, the scraping of the pupils was a painful affair to William, but he bore it bravely, and waited patiently for the visit of the surgeon to him again the next morning. He was thankful for the sleeping draught which they gave him, and woke next morning feeling rested and waiting with eager anticipation for the surgeon's report. When he received it, William was very quiet. The surgeon found that there was nothing that could be done to relieve William's condition. His blindness was indeed permanent and incurable, and must be endured.

'I am more sorry than I can say,' said the doctor to William, 'that I can do nothing for you. You have been a model patient. I wish you very well. What, by the way, do you do for a living, or is it not possible for you to manage that?'

William told him of his little blind school and of his work. He said that it was his intention to make the care of the blind his life's work.

'I feel, sir,' he told the surgeon, 'that this blindness of mine is not so much an affliction as an apprenticeship which I must serve in order to find out exactly what the needs of the blind are.'

The surgeon was very impressed by this remark. 'I respect your decision, my boy, and I shall try to follow your career as closely as I can.' He then shook hands with William and went his way.

At that moment Maria arrived with young Robert, ready to help her husband back to their lodgings where he could rest until next morning when they would have to be on their way back home.

Before they settled down that night, William took Maria in his arms.

'We are no worse off, my love, than we were before. In fact, I feel more determined than ever to embark upon the rest of my life's work, knowing that God has a plan, and that we shall fit into this. I am sorry that I can be of no better use to you, but I am still confident that all will be well.'

William's confidence and faith were about to be sorely tried yet again. When they reached home the next day, they were mortified to find that an order had been placed upon it. They were able to stay overnight, but next morning the officers arrived and took away all their possessions in lieu of rent. Maria was beside herself.

'Officer,' she cried to the man in charge, 'where am I to put the baby if you take away his cot? I pray you, leave us that. It is little to ask.'

The officer was sympathetic. 'I am only doing my job, Ma'am,' he said. 'I am sorry to have to do this to you, but I will leave the child's bassinette.'

Maria put the baby into it, and she and William walked sadly away. They walked slowly over to William's mother's, there to try to make some plans for their future.

It had been a sad blow to them both. But even then, in his secret heart, William felt that a way would be found.

III

William's mother's concern for William and Maria was very great. She did not let her son into her innermost thoughts, but she was secretly worried about him and his wife. When she had learned that they had taken a second house, as well as a shop, and that they were in such straits, she was desperately unhappy.

For some time, Mrs Moon had not been really well. She, herself, found life difficult, trying to make ends meet. She and her husband had never been wealthy in the smallest degree, and now, with the rent of her cottage, keeping both herself and her daughter when the latter was at home, brought her to the belief that matters would have to change if she was to be comfortable. Her doctor had recommended rest upon more than one occasion, when she had been subject to fainting and depression, but rest was not always possible.

She had always made a habit of keeping her home in an immaculate condition, sometimes doing small repairs which should more properly have been done by a labourer. She must take some definite action to try to restore her former health and contentment. Jane was now in full-time employment, looking after the old lady to whom she had read, and generally helped in the running of her house. She came home for an occasional day now, and this was easing her mother's burden to some extent.

When Mrs Moon learned of the latest misfortune of William and Maria, knowing full well that they had nowhere else to go, she made an application for a post in the town which she felt sure she could manage. If she were successful in obtaining the position, she would be a great deal better off financially. And she was more happy than she had been since William's marriage when she was appointed to the post for which she had applied. She knew now what she must do.

William was now homeless, and action was urgent. Therefore, Mrs Moon was very pleased indeed to see William and Maria. William afterwards said to Maria, she was sounding more cheerful, and brighter than he had heard for some time.

When they were all seated in the sitting room, and Mrs Moon had taken the baby upon her lap, she spoke.

'I am leaving this cottage, William, and I want you and Maria to move in at once.'

The young people were amazed. 'But where are you going?' they asked.

'There is a new boarding school opening next week, and I have been appointed housekeeper there.'

'But,' questioned William, 'are you well enough? Are you sure you can take this on?'

'Have no fear, William,' said his mother. 'I am looking forward to it tremendously. I shall have a roof over my head, under which I shall be paid for living. That is a very different situation from having to pay rent to live here. I shall be fed, housed, warmed, and very important this, occupied in something which I know I shall enjoy.

William and Maria were quite overcome. Maria went over to her mother-in-law and put her arms around her, giving her a kiss as she did so.

'How can we thank you, Mother? It is a quite miraculous release for William and me. Thank you, thank you.'

So it was that William, Maria and the baby, were able at once to move into the cottage, while their mother went to her new occupation with a cheerful heart and a great sense of relief at the outcome of these events.

As they retired for their first night in their mother's lodging, William took Maria's hand in his, and said, 'It is thus that we find God's goodness to us. I have every confidence that He will see us through.'

Maria raised his hand to her cheek. 'Your faith is greater than mine, but I do feel that we shall be led where He wishes us to go.' Maria was a devout woman, and, in spite of all she had so far undergone, she was content to await events, with William at her side.

William saw very little of his mother after she took the housekeeper's post at the school. A couple of brief visits were all that could be managed. Mrs Moon stayed only three years in her new position. She was taken ill with pneumonia in the Autumn term of her third year there, and died two weeks afterwards. She was greatly missed by all at the school for she had been a very popular figure there. Her friendly attitude caused everyone to take her to their hearts.

William and Maria felt her loss deeply, but, as William said, no doubt she was now restored to her husband, the loss of whom had lain so heavily upon her.

IV

Mrs Moon's rent was paid until the end of the next quarter, so William and Maria made the cottage their home until that time. On the evening before they were due to leave, William went out into the garden when it was dusk. He had enjoyed many happy hours in that garden during his youth, and he felt a sadness at the prospect of parting for ever from the beech tree which he had always loved. He made his way carefully towards the tree and, reaching upwards he caressed the lower branches, then laid his hand upon the grey-green bark.

'You have been a good friend to me, and a great comfort many times. I shall miss you. Thank you for having been such a constant friend.'

Saying which, he leant his head against the trunk for a moment before making his way carefully back to the house.

William's love of natural beauty had constituted a great part of his belief in God.

They had been able to find a small house into which they moved. They were blessed with good friends, and one in particular made them a present of sufficient money to enable them to furnish two rooms, giving them their first home, with their own belongings. William's salary at the time was still seven and sixpence a week, so no extra money could be found for any emergency.

In the Spring of the next year, William and Maria talked long about how they could augment their meagre income, and it was decided that they would again attempt to run a little shop, in the hope that any profit it might make would make life easier. This they did, with great hope.

Almost at once a new difficulty arose. Maria was expecting the birth of another child, and this added to their needs for funds. Then another blow fell. Their new landlord told William that he would have to raise their rent by another sixpence a week. It was difficult enough to find the two shillings which they were committed to, and William told the landlord that it was quite impossible for him to pay even a penny more.

As was William's habit, he took the matter into his prayers, and waited patiently for any improvement which might benefit them. He was not disappointed. Some weeks later, his salary was raised to ten shillings a week, and William gaily paid his landlord what was now due. 'It is,' said William to his wife, 'yet another instance of our lives being watched over by our heavenly Father.'

As the weeks wore on, although the little shop made some increase in their monetary affairs, it was very little. Maria was confined and their daughter was born. Then William found life exceedingly hard. He must take on all responsibility for the care of his wife, for there was no extra money whatsoever for paying for help. His daily routine was then a very full and hard one.

The day began at about four a.m. William would then, having had a short night's rest, get up and attend to his wife. He made breakfast for her, consisting of thin porridge, and a cup of tea. He dressed, washed and fed his son, and took a cup of tea himself, before cleaning up the fire grate and the rest of the room. Then his wife's room, and taking her anything she needed for herself and the baby, before setting out at nine o'clock for school.

By lunch time he was back at home, soon after mid-day, caring for his family and making sure that all was well before he should leave again for the afternoon session, which did not end until five o'clock. The evenings were long and arduous. By the time all was done, his wife and children settled for the night, and plans made for the following morning, William was exhausted, and retired to bed at about midnight, only to fall immediately into an exhausted sleep.

One morning, Maria was startled to hear from her bedroom, a great crash, and to smell the unmistakable odour of very hot water on a fire. She called out, and was more than relieved when William came to the foot of the stairs to explain that the kettle, full of boiling water, had fallen from the hob.

'But don't worry, my love. There's no harm done, and I have not even been touched by the water.' He then built up the fire, and placed the kettle very steadily upon the hob, before having to go out to start school.

This state of affairs continued for a week, and William was very relieved when it was found that Maria was well enough to be downstairs and to take charge of the household affairs.

Chapter 4

THE LACK OF MONEY was still a source of deep worry to them, but William kept his strong faith, and would not give way to it. He was more concerned with his other problem. This was how to teach his blind pupils more effectively.

One evening after both children were asleep, William and Maria sat talking. William turned towards his wife, imagining her dark beauty. Her steady eyes, with their affectionate expression, her soft hair turned up into a bun and tucked away in the little white cap she often wore. He was well content just to be with her, only wishing that he might be able to remove their monetary problems from her and wishing with all his heart that he could see her for himself and not rely upon what he had been told about her. Eventually he spoke...

'My love, I have been thinking a great deal lately about how best to help some of my pupils. They do not progress as I would wish, and they seem so frustrated.'

'What is your main problem, then,' asked Maria, 'and how do you think you might be able to cope with it?'

'I have prayed long and earnestly about it,' answered William, 'and I feel I must endeavour to find a simpler form of reading in order to get them to progress at all. This phonetic method which we are using is, as you know, the method I use myself, but it is far beyond the scope of some of these children. I have one particularly in mind.'

'Which would that be?' asked Maria, who knew many of the children.

'The little boy who has been with us since we began, and who, even before that, was trying to learn. He is, or appears to be, rather backward.'

'I know the one you mean. I have often spoken to him when I have been down to meet you. So what is to be done?'

With his usual faithful patience, William said he would continue to pray about the problem, upon which point they retired to bed.

Some days later, William thought he began to see a way out of this pressing problem. He told Maria that he thought he was being shown a method of reading which was going to be manageable by all.

This proved to be so, and after sitting up late on several nights, and writing down a note every time a constructive thought occurred to him, William went triumphantly to his wife to show her the page of characters he had developed. They were both delighted, and very excited at the possibilities of the scheme.

William produced a set of frames upon which he had arranged characters cut and shaped of copper wire, so that they were easily distinguishable by touch. He then began to teach it to the class. Imagine his delighted satisfaction when, after a very short time, the little boy who had been thought to be backward, began to read simple words from this new method.

The little boy in question was a changed character. He went home to his mother full of his achievement, and she, kind soul, was happier than she had been since her boy became blind.

William's satisfaction when he realised what might be the possibilities of his new raised letters, went about singing his favourite hymns at home, praising the Lord for all his mercies. For William, everything worked together for good to those who loved God. Even his sadness at not being able to see his dear wife and children seemed to have its place in the scheme of things.

In order to make use of his new alphabet, the raised type had to be made by manipulating copper wire in short lengths, bending it to the shape of the letters and fixing it to a tinned iron sheet. Then, when sentences were constructed, the sheet could be inverted over the paper, and an embossed result obtained.

It took many hours of hard work to produce these sheets, and William was up until very late at night, doing the work himself. Maria was always sympathetic, and gave all the help within her power, but it was William who had to carry most of the burden at first. He would creep into bed in the small hours, exhausted but happy, and his enthusiasm carried him along. He was more than delighted with the result.

One day a lady visitor was ushered into his classroom, showing the greatest interest in his work. Her visit was not repeated, however, and, although she promised that there would be some help, he heard no more of her for some time. Had he but known it, she was not idle, and was happy to talk to a great friend about William. Some time later, a gentleman visited the school, and it was through his conversation that William came to appreciate that the lady had been as good as her word. His visitor said, 'I have heard about your new method of raised letters for teaching the blind to read. The lady who told me came to visit you herself some time ago. The apparent delay in any action was caused by the fact that I have been travelling, and am only recently home again.'

William began to be more interested.

'I believe,' went on his visitor at last, 'that you would like to be able to produce your type for the benefit of the blind, not necessarily only children.' He looked keenly at William.

'That is most certainly true, sir,' said William. 'It is a difficult situation in which I find myself. The cost of putting my scheme into practice is, as far as I am concerned, quite prohibitive.'

'What do you estimate the cost to be, then?' asked the man.

'Oh, at least twenty pounds,' replied William. 'And that is a sum which I cannot even contemplate at present.'

'I am very impressed with the possibilities of your type,' said the visitor. And, as he was about to leave he gave William a donation of two pounds as a starter, saying that he would be back within two days.

After the visitor had left, William did not know what to think. He did not know who the gentleman was, and had never heard his name. He wondered what he should do with the two pounds left with him if the man did not return. He was to find out.

Two days later the same man returned, and William was quite overwhelmed to hear what he had to say.

'My friend, you will find twenty pounds at your disposal to start your work, and it gives me the greatest satisfaction to be able to do this for you. Your work is most valuable. There is one condition but I do not think it will be insuperable.'

'And what is that?' asked William.

'That you go to your school committee and lay the matter before them, asking for their agreement for you to teach this new system fully in your school.'

William agreed to this, and shook hands with his benefactor warmly, when he was leaving.

Without wasting time, William approached the committee the next day.

'And what can we do for you?' asked the chairman upon whom William had called.

William told him the whole story, and it was agreed that the chairman would call a meeting and that they would discuss the matter. A few days later they met, and, just before leaving school in the afternoon, William was called in.

'Well, Mr Moon,' said the chairman, 'we have discussed this matter, and we would like to hear a little more about the scheme from your own lips, here and now.'

William explained again, telling them of the great benefits he felt would obtain if he could be allowed to proceed with his own scheme. He was subdued as he sensed disapproval.

'If you will just wait a few minutes,' said the chairman, 'we will talk about what you have said, and call you back in under half an hour.'

William went back to finish putting away various items in his classroom. Just as he finished, the committee secretary came to his door and asked William if he would come back to the committee.

As soon as he entered the room, William's fears were realised. Although he himself knew that his scheme was superior to any that had yet been tried with the children, he had a feeling that it had not met with the approval of these men. He was right.

'We have talked this matter over carefully, Mr Moon, and we have had to come to the conclusion that we cannot agree to accepting your new alphabet for teaching at this school.'

William was deeply disappointed, and left the room with a heartache which he had not experienced since first he had formed his new reading method. What would now happen, he wondered?

Maria was comforting, and begged William to take heart. 'As you always tell me, dear,' she consoled him, 'there is a meaning to everything, and we shall come through this as well as through everything else which has befallen us.'

The next day William was surprised to receive another visit so soon from his benefactor. The gentleman was disturbed at William's news, but not for long.

'If you will allow me, Mr Moon, (and even if you will not), I shall take up this matter myself, and I shall see to it that the necessary sheets are prepared for producing your method, as this simple alphabet will benefit many blind people apart from those children in your class. We will work together.'

William was very surprised, yet full of gratitude. It mattered more to him that the blind should read, than that any committee should stand in the way of the production of his scheme.

It was not long before William heard from the benefactor again. The man had purchased type at his own expense, and then bought a wooden press in order to produce books. This was indeed a great opportunity for William to produce material for the benefit of the blind. There was one difficulty. The premises in which he was then living were too small to accommodate the necessary equipment, and for the work to be carried on. He had still his small shop, which had provided but little extra money, but now he must get rid of that, and move into larger premises.

The lack of funds was still their major concern, and it was hard indeed to make ends meet on William's salary of ten shillings a week. It must be remembered, however, that in the eighteen forties and fifties more provision could be made with less expenditure than would be the case a hundred years later. Maria was a good manager, and they bought only the more nourishing, albeit cheaper, foods.

The prospect of moving to other premises had its drawbacks, but was, even so, exciting. William would be able to progress with his embossing work as well as teaching, and the prospect was exhilarating.

William had never been happy that his benefactor still refused to reveal his name, and one day he asked the direct question.

'You may call me Charles, if it will make you happier,' came the reply, and so matters proceeded, although William was never quite content to be kept at arm's length. He certainly appreciated the great kindness and generosity of Mr Charles, and added his thanks to God in his prayers.

As soon as they found other accommodation, William began in earnest to put his embossing to good use. He worked as many hours as he could, sitting up late and rising early in order to put the press to good use. In addition to this he was still teaching at the school, and Maria was often anxious that her husband would collapse, so tired did he sometimes appear. She gave William all the help possible between caring for the children and running their home, but she found it exhausting at times, and her health suffered accordingly.

After some little time the landlady came to Maria and told her that she must really insist upon Mr Moon taking his press elsewhere. His late and very early hours, the noise of the press, and the general wear and tear upon her floors, all combined to make life well nigh intolerable for her. They would have to go.

Maria was in some distress when William returned home that afternoon after school. Naturally, he was very concerned, and asked her what the trouble was. When Maria told him what the landlady had said, William sighed.

'We have no choice but to find another place, my love,' he said, 'but do not let it become too much of a burden to you. I shall begin making enquiries immediately, and I shall put all the problem in my prayers tonight.'

William was as good as his word. The very next day he came home with news that he had been successful in finding other premises. They were to move within the week.

Accordingly, on the Wednesday following, William took some time from his teaching, leaving his class in the care of one of the church workers, and he and Maria set about packing up what few possessions that had. A small cart drew up outside the house, and the little family, with the help of the carter, packed it up and climbed aboard themselves, for the short journey to their new abode.

They settled in with their new landlady, and William again began his embossing work. Unfortunately, before long the press failed, and it was found that an iron one would have to be obtained. The wooden one had lost its strength and was useless.

Not knowing how to provide the money for such an expensive item as an iron press, William decided to have a subscription fund set up. People were very kind, and before long they had the necessary funds for purchasing the press. Maria having helped with some of the necessary collecting. She was to find herself many times in the future walking the streets of the town in order to collect donations for their work.

Another disappointment was in store for the Moons. When the landlady saw the iron press, she refused it admittance, saying that it was far too heavy an object to bring into her house. And again, they were obliged to move their lodgings.

The next apartment they were to take proved to be quite useless. They decided to take a whole house, but after moving in it was found to be as damp as to be almost wet. Dry rot was in the floors, and the walls ran with moisture. Both William and Maria as well as the children, were constantly catching severe colds. Added to all these drawbacks, owing to the dry rot in the floor of the room which housed the press, the foot of the press went through.

The Moon family moved yet again.

When Mr Charles heard of this latest catastrophe in the Moon family, he told William firmly that he had a proposition to make. He would buy a house himself, and then the Moons could rent from him and move in, with their iron press. This he did, and it was with thankful hearts that William and Maria found themselves under a reliable roof, much to their satisfaction. There was, however, one problem. The expense of this house, with rent and other charges, amounted to twenty two pounds per annum, a figure which they had not before had to contend with. Fortunately, William at about this time, received an increase in his salary from the school of four shillings a week. This would be a help, at least.

More help was soon to be at hand for William and Maria, although it was to prove not as beneficial as they had hoped. Maria's father died, and in his will, left his daughter the sum of twenty five pounds per year. No doubt he had repented of his unco-operative ways when she married William, and thought to make some sort of amends. It certainly appeared, on the face of it, that at least, William and his wife would be solvent, and to spare.

This was not to be. Their rent was raised, they had had to give up the little shop which William had opened a year or two before, owing to the amount of work with which he was now faced, so that by and large, they were only slightly better off than previously. William did not despair. His complete and absolute faith in God's plans, gave him all the confidence he needed, even though, in his human frailty, there were times when he could have wished for better things for Maria.

William's work of embossing and printing for the blind brought in no financial benefits to him, and they were obliged to carry on with their daily work in the hope that matters could only improve.

The early Spring had seen the Moon family settled in their new home, and in April of eighteen forty nine they had completed the embossing of several of the Gospels. There had been, as soon as the new mode of reading began to be known, a great demand for the Scriptures. This delighted William's heart, as he set great store by the word of God, and wished for as many of the blind population to be able to read it as possible. In that area of the South of England at that time no provision was made for giving assistance to the blind. They were not taught to read, or use their hands, and it was beginning to be plain to William that he must put forth every effort if he was to bring the benefit he so desired, to the blind.

The many vicissitudes of their lives which they endured did not make William unhappy. Indeed, he told his wife one day that he could not be happier. His deep faith was so unlifting to him; his wife and children so dear, and the possibility of his being able to do the great work for the blind which he felt he had been called upon to undertake, gave him a serenity of spirit which nothing could shake.

Chapter 5

WILLIAM'S SERENITY OF SPIRIT was infectious, and all with whom he came into contact were enriched. His children adored him, and the little family were never happier than when they could find an hour to be together. Sometimes, William would deliberately call a halt to his heavy work load, when he and Maria would take the children down to the sea shore, there to search excitedly in pools for the small creatures inhabiting them.

The occasions were rare, but William felt it essential that they should occur. Life, although filled with a rather hectic work load, was for living. Any pleasure, however small, in which the whole family could take part, was fundamental in the bringing up of the children.

As the embossing progressed, William became well known for his philanthropic attitude, his kindness, and above all for the great benefits which he was able to bring to the blind. He began a monthly magazine for the blind, and it was in this connection that an incident took place at about that time.

After school was finished one day, William was surprised to receive a visit there from a blind man accompanied by his sister. They all walked over to William's house, and there the lady noticed a copy of William's monthly magazine. She was attracted to its title.

'A Magazine for the Blind,' she read aloud. 'That is something new.' She passed it over to her brother commenting upon its unusual appearance. As her brother took the magazine in his hands, he began to trace the outlines of the embossed type.

'This is quite remarkable, Mr Moon,' he said. 'I can clearly feel the letters of these words, and read the content.'

'It is embossed in my original script,' explained William. 'I find that people are beginning to read exceptionally well from it.'

'You are right, sir,' replied the blind man. 'I find this by far the easiest and most manageable type that I have yet met, and I am very impressed by it.'

'We are about to embark upon embossing the Scriptures,' said William. 'This will take a very long time, and cost a great deal of money, but I look forward to the day when the Bible is available for the blind.'

'Mr Moon,' said the man slowly. 'I am interested, very interested. If you will accept it, I would like to make an initial donation towards the work.'

'That is extremely generous of you, sir,' said William. 'I will most certainly accept any donation from anyone who is sufficiently concerned that this work should go ahead.'

Before they left, William received a generous gift from the blind visitor, who continued his support for some considerable time.

The work of producing the Scriptures in full, then began.

William's fame began to spread. Apart from his school, he was involved in visiting and teaching blind people in their own homes. Although sometimes quite exhausted, he kept on with his good works, filling any free moments with the work on the Scriptures. Subscriptions were necessary, and Maria found herself walking many miles through the town, collecting the money which had been promised. She was ever very supportive of her husband, and worked hard in whatever way came along, to help him. She was a devout woman, and it was to their mutual comfort that they shared all the work as far as possible, feeling that they were doing God's will.

Robert was now a little boy of about five years old, and his sister, affectionately called 'Adele', about a year younger. Naturally they took up a good deal of their mother's time and energies, but, even when Maria was more than usually busy helping with the embossing and collecting, they were never neglected. They were a happy family. Although money was never in great supply, they were finding life a little easier than formerly.

At about that time there was another incident of the greatest interest to William.

Attention was being drawn to the existence of many blind people in other parts of the world, and it came to William's ears that China was particularly affected in this way. William was acquainted with a certain clergyman whom he thought, or rather, knew, would have knowledge of conditions in other countries. China was uppermost in William's mind. He had, as always, put the matter in his prayers, and felt confident that he must now go ahead with an idea which kept returning to his mind. He wrote to the clergyman who was the Secretary to the British and Foreign Bible Society, telling him of his intention of trying to supply some embossed reading to the blind in China.

A couple of days later, William was surprised to receive a visit from the clergyman, the Rev. Mr Brendren, and that he had come to find a Mr Moon who had written to him about a projected Chinese mission. Although the two gentlemen had corresponded on previous occasions, they had never met.

William admitted to being Mr Moon, and the clergyman was invited in.

Maria entered the room with them, enquiring whether Mr Brendren might like some refreshment.

'Thank you, no,' was the answer. 'I have but a few moments ago enjoyed a snack in the hotel. But I thank you, ma'am, for the thought.'

When they were all seated, the clergyman said to William, 'I understand that you are interested in helping the blind in China in some way.'

'Most certainly I am.' replied William. 'I feel sure that it is within my power to bring help by means of my embossed books, to those blind in that country, as well as anywhere else.'

'Forgive me, sir,' said the clergyman. 'It occurs to me that it is rather presumptuous of you to assume that you could do this. How would you cope with the language?'

'Of course, I would learn it,' replied William confidently.

'It is a quite outlandish language, Mr Moon. How would you set about it? And what else would you require in order to set this project in hand?'

'Two things, sir,' replied William. 'Money for the expenses of the printing, and a Chinese dictionary.'

The clergyman laughed aloud. 'You certainly have the gift of confidence, Mr Moon. I admire your strength of mind.'

After a little more general conversation, the clergyman said he must take his leave, promising to be in touch with William again shortly. He was as good as his word.

Only two days later, William received a cheque for twenty five pounds from the British and Foreign Bible Society, and a parcel of several volumes of a Chinese dictionary.

William was delighted and began immediately to study the language, Maria helping him with the descriptions of the letters and words he would require. Not long after, William was able to construct a few sentences using his own simplified alphabet into the Chinese. He felt sure that any blind person who came to use it, would find it simple, and crisp to the touch.

The Secretary of the Bible Society had been talking about William and his project to his colleagues in London.

'A most remarkable character, this William Moon,' he said. 'I was very impressed with his determination, although I did feel that he was attempting the impossible, to translate into Chinese in his embossed type.'

'I would rather like to visit this gentleman,' said a colleague. 'Did you say he was in Brighton?'

'That is so. He lives in a house with its own workshop for the printing work. He has an attractive wife, too, a quiet woman, but as determined as her husband, I would say, to promote her husband's ideas. Yes, go and visit them, by all means.'

Thus advised, his colleague set out next day for Brighton. The train journey was of great interest to him, as he had never yet been any distance at all by rail.

Not being acquainted with the town, he enquired of a passer by where he might find Mr Moon's house.

'Oh, you're not far from it,' responded the woman. 'Everyone knows where William Moon lives. He's a fine man, and his work for the blind is now well known.' And she directed him to the Moon dwelling.

Arriving there and knocking upon the door, William's new visitor was ushered in by Maria, who went to fetch William from the workshop where he was busy on a piece of the Scriptures. William shook hands with his visitor who then said, 'I understand from my colleague in London that you are attempting to produce some embossed reading for the blind in China.'

'That is so,' said William. 'Have you then some further knowledge?'

'I have a Chinese acquaintance, and I wondered whether you might like to meet him? I am sure he would be interested in what you are attempting.'

'That would be splendid! Do bring him here whenever you can. I shall be delighted to make his acquaintance.'

When the Chinese gentleman had made William's acquaintance, he was impressed with what he heard and saw, and immediately offered, if William was willing, to assist in the work. William of course was happy with the suggestion, and the two went to work whenever they could get together. After a short time, William was excited by the fact that he had been able to produce the Lord's Prayer and a piece of Scripture, in the colloquial language of Peking. Maria was told of this, and, that evening just before bedtime, she told her son an exciting story of how his clever father was going to be able to help blind people as far away as China. Young Robert took in all this information, and it began to lay the foundations for his later interests, and participation, in his father's great work.

There was no little excitement in the Moon household as the script was packed up and sent to the missionary station in China. The missionary in charge was a Miss Alders, who, when she had examined William's production, sent back a message to England giving her approbation and warm thanks to William. She requested him to produce a part of her church liturgy, and of gospel, to be used in the missionary station for teaching some of the blind people attending there. William was delighted to be able to do this immediately, and before many weeks were past, he sent off the completed script. Most of the expense of preparing this material for the Chinese blind was met by a benefactor who gave William the funds for what was required. This same benefactor was so generous on future occasions, that William's work benefitted to the extent of more than a hundred pounds. William told his wife that the world was full of kindness and generosity, with which she had to agree. Their world certainly seemed so. It was the encouraging assistance given to William's work which gave him so much quiet satisfaction. As usual, he and his wife gave thanks in their evening prayers for all God's goodness to them.

II

As time went on and William's output from his workshop grew, he began to turn his mind to work further afield.

'You know, my love,' he said to Maria one day, 'I feel I must travel about a little further and see what can be done for all those blind who at present have no source of succour.'

'That is very noble of you, William,' replied Maria. 'I feel that you are right, as you most usually are. I will do all I can to support you.'

'That goes without saying, my dear. You have always been my inspiration and my help. I trust that you appreciate that fact.' He kissed his wife, and went away to the workshop.

It was then that the acquaintance with a benevolent lady whose name was Graham, began to mature. She was a very devoted worker in the cause of the blind, travelling far and wide up and down the country seeking out such, and making sure that they received whatever help they needed.

Eventually, William joined forces with Miss Graham and, between them, they set up a workshop and school for blind children, where they were taught the art of basket making as well as learning to read. Those making use of the place included those other than children. The benefits of being able to read were greatly appreciated and it was a very sad day when, later, the workshop had to be closed due to lack of sufficient accommodation for the basketwork they produced. But the teaching continued by visiting. Indeed, some days William and his helper were occupied twelve hours a day, feeling desperately tired when it was time to go home.

After such a beginning, it was not surprising that William's co-worker should spend so many years travelling the country, doing everything within her power to bring comfort to the blind.

At home, William continued with what he regarded as his life's mission, and the embossing successfully completed, by the end of eighteen fifty one, the New Testament and the Book of Psalms were completed, together with the Book of Isaiah. These constituted a great amount of material, and the cost had been met by subscriptions as before. William also decided to emboss pictures, producing outlines of various animals for the sake of those who had never seen one. He also produced a certain amount of music which was acclaimed with delight by those who needed to be able to use it.

The subscriptions for the year had covered the expenses of materials, one or two workpeople, and the running of the workshop housed in the ground floor of their home. Maria had spent many hours walking, collecting as she had done before, the necessary funds to cover William's projects. The work was becoming well known and much in demand, and Maria was glad to be able to contribute her efforts to the required end. She had been so cheerful about doing this tiring chore, and the effort was beginning to take its toll on her health. Several times she suffered great weariness and severe chills, and this caused William great concern. As soon as she recovered from each set-back, however, Maria was determined as ever to continue with her task.

Apart from the daily teaching and production of script, William had concentrated upon translating his alphabet into no less than six foreign languages, so that his embossed type might be read in other countries. This, however, was only a beginning, for some years later there were no less than one hundred and ninety four different languages in use. William Moon was fulfilling his vow to bring sight to the blind, at least as far as reading was concerned. It was, also, his greatest comfort to be able to produce the Bible so that others could obtain the comfort from its reading, that he himself did.

In spite of Maria's determination to do everything she could to forward William's plans, she was again taken ill with what the doctor thought looked remarkably like exhaustion. Doctor Hanson was still their family doctor, as he had been William's and his mother's ten years before. He was beginning to think of retirement, but was a very present help in trouble to many, even as he approached his seventieth birthday.

Maria was flushed, yet felt cold. The doctor felt her pulse, and, still with her wrist in his hand, he said, 'What are the chances of your getting a hot drink, preferably with some whisky in it?'

Maria smiled faintly. 'I'm afraid there is nothing alcoholic in the house, doctor. Perhaps you have forgotten that we do not keep any; in fact, we never use it.'

'Hot lemon them, or some broth? I think you need something really warming inside you.'

He put down Maria's hand. 'You have a severe chill, m'dear,' he told her. 'Have you been out collecting again in the wet weather we seem to have lately?'

'Well, yes, I have,' answered Maria. 'I was out yesterday and the day before. You know it is necessary that I do this. Our last subscriptions are used up, and William needs to replenish.'

'William must replenish his own subscriptions for a bit, then. You are to stay in bed for three days, and I'll look in again on the fourth. I insist that you have rest and warmth. How will you manage about the children?'

'William will look after them, doctor, and they can go into the workshop so long as there is somebody there to see that they do no harm. We shall manage.'

'I know your "managing",' smiled the doctor, rather grimly. You are to do exactly as I say this time. I will see William as I go out, and give him some orders.'

The doctor then shook hands with Maria and left the room, glancing back at the attractive if rather flushed countenance on the pillows. She was quite beautiful, he thought, and one of the really good women I'm glad to meet. He went in search of William, and, telling him what he had just told Maria, and giving instructions that she must rest, he left the house.

Whenever an interruption such as the present one occurred in the work, William never lost his patience. Maria must be looked after. So he prepared to make the extra effort it would need, and fit in his work with Maria's needs.

When Doctor Hanson next called, Maria was greatly improved. The children, said William, had been extremely helpful, carrying small things up to their mother with the exaggerated care which small children use in such circumstances. They felt very important when called upon to help, and Robert said he was a bit sorry that his mother was coming downstairs now. William and Maria smiled affectionately, as parents will. Maria was back in their midst, and all would be well.

William was glad to get back to their normal arrangements, but his concern was greater than before Maria's illness. The subscriptions were in need of renewal, and he was anxious to begin the new year with a clean sheet as regarded his monetary affairs. On the other hand, he felt a certain rightness in his situation. He had often said that his blindness was an apprenticeship which he must serve in order to appreciate fully what it meant to those so afflicted.

He felt similarly on the subject of poverty. He was quite sure that, in order to appreciate exactly the position of the poor, he must serve a similar apprenticeship in that way himself, in order to experience what it was really like to have insufficient money adequately to pay his way. So he approached the new year with renewed faith, confident that his way would be made plain to him.

Nevertheless, William had to admit that he had lately been troubled because of scurrilous rumours put about by some people that he supported his family upon the subscriptions and the small amount of profit. The profit which had accrued over the past two years had amounted to less than ten pounds, and this was ploughed back into the work. He was glad of the assistance of his great friend who kept his accounts. William knew that there could be no vestige of truth in any of these rumours. Maria told him that it arose from jealousy on the part of those people who could not endure to see a success being made of anything at all, and William was not to worry any more about it. Anyone who really mattered, she told him, and who understood what was involved in his work, fully appreciated the position, and nobody else mattered.

In the Summer of eighteen fifty one, William took Maria and the children to the Great Exhibition. They toured the many stands of exhibits and at the display of Scriptures, books, and general information about what was being done for the disabled, particularly the blind, William was gratified to be told that he had done more to promote the welfare of the blind than any other person up to that date. Maria was very proud of him and pointed out to the children that Papa was becoming quite famous, but that they must not be conceited about it.

Life at the moment was very sweet, and Maria went back home full of joy at the prospect of their doing even more to help the unfortunate blind people. She intended, when they were back home, to start again the collecting for the next subscriptions.

Chapter 6

WHEN WILLIAM HAD FIRST INVENTED his new method of reading by touch, and had printed his first booklet, he little thought that his labours would benefit thousands of blind people all over the world. He was a modest man, but determined to work entirely for the blind. More than once he had said to his wife, 'I feel, in fact, I know that this work has been given to me because I am myself blind.' Even then, although he was to open the door of the world of books to many of his countrymen and women, he did not envisage the extent to which his concern would take him.

One result of his endeavours had been the formation of the Brighton School for Blind Boys, but, not content with his local successes, he felt he must travel further afield, with the intention, if at all possible, of starting schools and libraries in other parts of the country.

William's fame was spreading, and one day he was told that a royal visitor was to come to his school. William was rather surprised, since it had not then occurred to him that he was doing anything spectacular. He was surprised to receive the Duchess of Gloucester. She was most impressed by what she saw, and having examined William's easier script, so clear to the touch and so rewarding to those who learned from it, that she commented that it was a great pity that this had not been invented a few years before, when her father and sister could have benefitted so much from it. She left the school, prepared to make William's achievement known to a wider circle. When William had told Maria of this visit, she was pleased for him, but she was fully aware that her modest husband would say no more about it.

While they were talking of this visit, and discussing in general terms how William thought the work was progressing and whether it would, or should lead to taking it further afield, he broached to her his desire to go to the North of England, where, he said, he understood that the needs of education and help for the blind was very great. Maria asked him whether he had ever talked to Miss Graham about this. William said that he had, and he knew that she travelled extensively in the course of her own intensive work for the blind.

'Well, the London Home Teaching Society seemed to be successful, my dear,' said William. 'I feel that there is a great need for other groups to be formed.'

'There is still a great deal of work to be done on the printing of the Bible, dear,' put in Maria. 'I would not wish you to take on a greater burden. If what is undertaken is truly worthy, then all should be well.'

Maria felt that her husband had already made up his mind that he must carry his work to a wider area. She also knew that she was willing to give any help within her power.

So it was that in the course of the next few years, Maria was called upon to take responsibility for the work, as well as her home and children, during William's quite frequent absences. The privations of their early married life, when they had had to go without sufficient food so many times, had left their mark upon Maria's health and strength. She gladly undertook to do everything she could to help her husband, and there is no doubt that, because of her own faith in what she also considered God's will, that the work should prosper, she often undertook collecting missions when she should have been resting. She, as well as William, was looking forward to the day when the printing of the Bible should be accomplished. But what would be the cost to herself?

It was in those years of the eighteen fifties that William undertook his missions up and down the country. He was personally responsible for inspiring people in so many parts of the provinces, notably, Yorkshire, to set up teaching societies for the blind. The home teaching for the blind was started! People gladly responded.

The man who had been responsible for encouraging William by his great generosity, Sir Charles Lowther, had become a great friend of William's. They shared similar ambitions, and because Sir Charles enjoyed the means whereby he could finance much of William's work, the work flourished.

A notable example of that generosity gave great joy to William himself. Many benefitted from Sir Charles's gift of embossed books to stock the lending libraries for the blind. Sir Charles was himself a Yorkshireman, and he felt that, in providing these books he was giving back to his fellow countrymen that which they had lost through blindness. His philanthropic attitude was greatly appreciated in the county, and their benefactor was highly esteemed.

Eventually, after much travel and visiting those whom he thought might be called upon to help, William had established no less than eighty teaching societies for the blind.

Returning home after one such occasion, William told Maria how thankful he was that he had followed his desires, and visited so many places in the interests of the blind. He talked about his friend Lowther, and it was then that he was able to tell his wife that in those earlier days, when an unidentified benefactor had come forward to their help, it had been none other than Sir Charles. No doubt, Lowther was more particularly interested in William's efforts, because he himself was also blind. It had been his mother who had first taught William to read from the existing scripts when first it became known that he had lost his sight.

'God moves in a mysterious way, Maria,' he said. 'We have found this to be true. Events are turning out to be so much more successful than ever I dreamed.'

That night, before retiring, they knelt together and gave thanks.

One day, in great excitement, William went to find Maria, who was busy in her kitchen preparing a meal.

'Come at once!' announced William.

'Why, William, what's amiss?' asked his wife.

'Nothing's amiss, my love, but I want you to be present in the workshop within the next ten minutes.'

Maria finished what she was about, and followed William, in some mystification, to the workshop where there seemed to be a feeling of excitement in the air. What could it be?

There were two or three workpeople at the press, and one who was just about to draw out a newly embossed sheet.

'Everybody stand back!' the operator of the press announced. 'You are about to see a miracle!'

Gathering round the press, William and Maria and the other workers felt wonderment. William was the only exception. He obviously must know what was about to happen. Then it happened.

'My friends,' said the press operator, removing a large sheet of embossed type from the rollers, 'this is the last piece of work to complete the embossing of the Bible. It has taken us ten years, and now we have achieved it.'

They all clapped, and William, taking the sheet from the operator's hands, could well have wept with relief and emotion.

'God be praised,' cried William. 'I think this is the moment when we give thanks for such an achievement. 'Well done all of you. Today I am a proud and thankful man.'

There was a short silence and Maria felt the tears gathering behind her eyes. She let them fall, and gave thanks with the rest.

'What a day!' cried William on their return home. William had sent the workers home for the rest of that day, and he and Maria, as ever, knelt together with thankful prayer.

II

William's next venture was to travel on the Continent in order to establish his methods there.

Both children were by now in their teens. Robert was growing fairly tall like his father, with the same dark colouring and upright figure. Adele had her mother's direct looking grey eyes and soft hair inclined to curl. They were an attractive pair, and their parents were proud of them. Yet even now, Maria often thought how good it would be if their father could only see them. This thought was to be with her all her life; she never ceased to regret that their home, although familiar to him now, and above all, their children, were a closed book to William. How often William himself might feel the need to see them all, was never revealed, but it would not be surprising if it occurred to William more often than he would admit.

Robert was now fourteen, and his father decided that he was old enough to accompany him as companion and guide on certain continental trips which he planned to make. Maria was consulted as usual, and she being willing to remain at home with Adele, and to keep an eye on the embossing, it was agreed that William and Robert start on a journey to Germany and Holland in order to encourage the institutions for the blind to make use of his simple method of reading.

In order to cross the Channel it was necessary to travel to London and embark from there. Robert was young enough to be excited at the prospect of an unaccustomed train journey to be topped with a boat trip. He was eager to set out, and found it irksome to have to help his father to pack up some scripts which they intended to take, to show to their continental friends. At last, however, the moment arrived. Maria and Adele went with them to the station and Maria begged Robert to take particular care of his father. Robert reassured his mother, said goodbye to her and his sister, and saw his father safely seated in the train.

Adele was a little disappointed as she walked back home with her mother.

'Why can't I go, Mama?' she asked.

'That would never do, Adele. Your father and Robert have gone on business, and the places they will visit would not be the most enjoyable of jaunts for you.'

William and Robert were on board the ship. It was one of the early steam boats, although still equipped with sail. Robert was full of curiosity, leaning over the side in order to see whatever was to be seen, and describe to his father what was going on. They then went below where special arrangements had been made for the blind man and his son. Their baggage had been stowed away, and they were free to enjoy the trip. Fortunately, the sea was sufficiently calm to make the journey pleasantly comfortable, and when they docked late that night on the other side, Robert and William both felt that they had had a short holiday.

The next morning Robert was kept busy describing to his father all that he saw. The people, the architecture, any countryside through which they passed were all new to the boy, and he did his utmost to help his father to 'see' them.

They visited the headquarters of the societies for the blind which they called upon. William had taken examples of his embossing type and copies of his alphabet, assuring his listeners that these could be made available in translations. Most of the officials were amazed at what William said could be done, and many of them undertook to take up William's offer. After this first visit, it became quite natural for William and his son to tour such continental places as already had set up these institutions for helping the blind.

William was very impressed by the reception his mission received. Both the Dutch and the Germans showed great interest, and it was not long before copies of passages from the Scriptures, and of the Lord's Prayer, were in the hands of the foreign institutions.

On their return home, Robert was full of his adventures, and regaled his mother and Adele with descriptions of the two countries they had visited.

'You know, Mother,' he said, sitting down to a bowl of her excellent soup, 'I believe Papa is getting quite famous. Most of the people we met seemed to have heard of him, although I can't think how.'

His mother admonished him slightly. 'Fame is not a good thing in itself, son. Your father is much too modest to find any pleasure in it. Yet I must admit that I am delighted to learn that his work is going before him in this way.'

Robert regarded his mother thoughtfully... 'You are right, Mama, as usual. I do understand that your own and Papa's modesty won't let you accept praise. Nevertheless, you must be glad that he is being so successful. Think of the many hundreds of people that he has helped already.' Robert was growing up.

Some two years later those concerned with working for the blind in Rotterdam, asked William if he could possibly help them to print their own books. William was again delighted, as he so often was when any success in the work proved itself to be showing results. He at once set the necessary arrangements in motion. In the course of the next few weeks, a press was ordered, and the embossed type made ready with a supply of the special paper. Then William, again with Robert's help, set sail for Holland.

The crossing this time was rather rough, and William sent Robert to make sure that the press was safe. He envisaged it being dragged away from its moorings, although the crew had assured him that it was well packed. All was well, however, and when the passage was over, the captain himself assured William that his men had landed the press quite safely.

Arriving in Rotterdam later that afternoon, William and Robert, with the help of some of the workers in the blind institute, set up the press in a large workroom, and, before retiring, William had a piece of embossed work ready for them to examine. The recipients were more than satisfied with what they saw, and there was a spirit of elation in the atmosphere that night.

Robert told his father that he should be very proud of such an achievement. 'Just think, Papa,' he said, 'these blind people will now have their own books printed, on their own premises, and it is all due to you.'

'My son,' said his father, 'I am truly thankful that we have been able to help them in this way, but we must remember that it is all God's doing, and it is His purpose upon which we are embarked.'

During the next year or two, the work went ahead. William's simple method was taking hold upon people's imagination, and he was called upon to travel many miles over the country, talking and demonstrating, until his work was known throughout the land.

It was at this time that William was to experience more concern about his wife's health.

Maria had, of late, shown signs of great weariness, and had had two or three attacks of the exhaustion which she had suffered so often before.

Doctor Hanson had retired, and his practice had been taken over by a younger man, very friendly and competent. William sent for him on the day that he found Maria collapsed beside the bed. Adele was fetched from the kitchen where she had been helping to prepare the mid-day meal. She and William between them raised Maria and made her as comfortable as they could on the bed. Then the doctor arrived.

Doctor Brent was a striking figure of a man. Six feet tall, fair-haired and handsome, he looked, thought Adele, rather like a Viking. After he had examined Maria thoroughly, he turned to William and said, 'I fear your wife is really ill.'

William was immediately all concern, and Adele looked scared.

'What do you think is the cause, doctor?' asked William.

'Overstrain, I think, Mr Moon. She will have to have a complete rest. No walking about, no exertion of any kind. This I insist upon.'

'I shall insist upon it, also,' said William. 'We must see to it that my wife is given every attention.'

'Are you able to get extra help at all?' asked Doctor Brent.

'I will see to it. My daughter will be able to do a great deal of course, and between us, the three of us will manage to do what is necessary.'

Maria had fallen asleep during this conversation, and William wondered how she was looking. As though in answer to his unspoken question, Doctor Brent told him that although very tired, his wife had a good colour and appeared comfortable. William was very thankful for this information and felt reassured. He asked the doctor whether there would be any medicine prescribed.

'Yes, I am going to send her a bottle containing a little morphia. This will help her to rest completely. Can one of you come to the surgery to collect it?'

Adele spoke eagerly. 'I will come, doctor. I can be there as soon as you think it should be ready.'

The doctor looked at Adele, liking what he saw. He told her to come at three o'clock that afternoon, and he would be there himself to give her any instructions.

They then all left the bedroom, leaving Maria to enjoy a much needed sleep.

As the time approached for her to set out for the surgery, Adele put on her coat and bonnet, feeling not a little sense of excitement at the thought of seeing this young giant again.

As she rang the surgery bell, Adele felt her colour rising a little. She told herself that she was on an urgent message, of great importance to her mother, and that any other thought must be dismissed from her mind. The door opened and she went inside.

Doctor Brent met Adele at the door of his surgery. Adele remembered it from the days of Doctor Hanson, when she had visited it occasionally with her mother. The room had not altered, but the doctor in charge most certainly had. As she shook hands with the doctor, Adele was aware of a feeling of security by the strong grip.

Pulling forward a chair, he asked Adele to sit down.

'Does your mother appear to be more rested, Miss Moon?' he enquired.

'She was still asleep when I left home,' replied Adele. 'She must be very tired indeed. I have never known her to take any rest at this time of day before.'

'I'm afraid she is thoroughly exhausted, and it will take a considerable time for her to be back on her feet. I have prepared this medicine for her. I want you to give it to her in the late evening today, and then half a dose at mid-day after food, repeating the nightly dose as for today. But the instructions are written on the bottle.'

'Thank you, Doctor Brent,' said Adele. 'I feel, we all feel, that she is in safe hands so long as you are taking care of her.'

'You are very kind, Miss Moon. You can rest assured that I shall keep a very close eye upon your mother. I will be in again tomorrow morning.'

Adele left the surgery feeling happier about her mother, and quite convinced that in Doctor Brent they had a champion who would do everything in his power for their invalid.

Adele prepared supper for her father and Robert that evening, taking up to her mother a small bowl of a nourishing, but thin, broth. This, she thought, would be easy for her mother to take, and she knew that it was a favourite of hers. Perhaps things would look a little better in the morning, after her mother had had a night's rest which the medicine should ensure.

When the doctor arrived next day, however, he shook his head after taking his patient's pulse and temperature.

Adele, watching, felt what a comfort it was to have this doctor in attendance upon her mother. She had always liked old Doctor Hanson, and had been sorry as was her father, when he had eventually decided to retire. But this pleasantly mannered young man, with his kindly attitude and friendly smile, gave her great confidence. She also had to admit to herself that she was aware of a pleasantly warm, confident feeling in his presence. Surely all would now be well.

Doctor Brent left the sickroom accompanied by Adele, whom he then asked to go and bring her father. Adele looked at him in some surprise.

'I think he is in the workshop, Doctor Brent, but I know he will want to see you before you go. I'll fetch him.' She took the doctor into their sitting room and went away.

William was just a little surprised to hear Adele's message. 'Of course, I'll come at once. I did not know that Doctor Brent had yet arrived.'

Back in the sitting room, when the young man rose to his feet, William bade him sit down again, when they all three did so. William was concerned.

'Mr Moon,' began Doctor Brent, 'I have asked particularly to see you now, because I fear I have some grave news.'

William drew in his breath sharply. Adele turned in her chair to face the doctor. 'What is it,' she whispered.

'I am more sorry than I can tell you, to have to say this, sir. I must be quite honest with you, however, and it is my duty, unpleasant though it is, to prepare you for what I know will be a shock.'

Adele rose and went to stand very near to her father. She rested her hand upon his shoulder, as they listened.

'Mr Moon, Miss Moon,' said the doctor. 'I fear that Mrs Moon is very seriously ill. I will do everything I can for her, but I fear you will have to prepare yourselves for an event which I'm sure you did not anticipate at this stage.'

'You mean she will not live?' said William.

'As I have said, sir, I shall do everything in my power to bring her back to health, but I must admit that it certainly appears that she is in a far worse condition than anyone realised.'

William put out a shaking hand. Adele took it and pressed it between her own. 'How long?' was the question in both their minds.

William found it too difficult to put his thoughts into actual words. Adele it was who pressed Doctor Brent to be more specific.

'I cannot forecast anything definite, sir. I can only tell you that your wife is dangerously ill. Will you allow me to procure a nurse, at least for a time?'

Adele intervened. 'I can take care of Mama, Doctor Brent.'

William turned towards the doctor, who shook his head slightly in Adele's direction.

'I am sure you will do whatever you can, Miss Moon, but I think it will be wiser to have a nurse in attendance for a few hours a day, at least.'

'And what about the night?' asked Adele.

'I am hoping that the morphia will help your mother to sleep for several hours during the night. This would not only be very beneficial to her, but it would enable the rest of you to take your proper rest, as well.'

'What you have told us,' said William, 'had been a great shock. I appreciate your openness, and thank you for it, but I'm sure you will appreciate that we have received a most unexpected blow today.'

'I appreciate it only too well, Mr Moon,' replied Doctor Brent. 'I felt that you would not wish me to be less than truthful. I will be back here this evening at about eight, if that will be convenient for you.'

Adele put out her hand to the doctor. He took it and held it firmly as he shook it. 'Thank you, Doctor Brent, for all your kindness and consideration. We will expect you back this evening.'

Doctor Brent was then shown out, and Adele followed her father up to her mother's bedroom. As soon as she looked in, she retreated: her father was on his knees at his wife's bedside, his hands clasped in prayer.

At that moment, Robert came home, returning from some mission which he had undertaken for his father. Adele met him at the door, and told him all that had passed during the past hour. The young man was shocked, and said he must go up at once to see his mother. Adele restrained him, telling him what she had just seen. The brother and sister then sat down together in order to discuss whatever action they should take.

The next few days were as a nightmare to the Moon family. That their mother should have been taken so unexpectedly ill was almost unbelievable to the two young people. Robert was now a man of twenty and his sister a little younger. They had never known of the deprivations of their parents in their early married life, as their father did. He was now only too well aware of the strain which his wife had endured, really for his sake. She had never stinted in giving him her help, and, although before the children were born, she had been near to breakdown from the distresses of their situation, she had done her best to keep her worries to herself. Was all that, William asked himself, the root cause of her many illnesses during the past two or three years? Although she had not always entirely confided in him in order to prevent him from worrying, he knew that she must have been in a state of extreme tension during that time. Now, he was feeling guilty, in spite of the fact that they had always had a close union of spirit throughout their married life. Whatever the basic cause of Maria's failing health, he must now put forth every endeavour to see that everything possible would be done to help her. He and the children together would have to fight this battle.

A nurse was appointed, and she, kindly soul, with motherly care added to her proficiency, did her utmost to care for the family. In this she was very successful, and her kindness was deeply appreciated by them all.

William forced himself to attend to the workshop and to fulfil any engagements which he had already made. He was much in demand by various groups to talk to them about his work for the blind, and he felt certain that, had Maria known, she would have been firmly of the opinion that he must not let down any of these people. Robert was a great help to his father, and Adele did stout work, keeping the house in order and seeing to it that her father and brother were well fed.

There then came a day which, whilst on the surface they had all appeared cheerful, had been at the back of all their minds, threatening the happiness of the whole family as well as that of many good friends who had been supporting them during this time.

Adele went up to see her mother one afternoon, when the nurse was having some free time, and, as soon as she saw her mother's face, she fled in terror down to the workshop to find her father.

William came running, his limbs trembling as he ran stumbling over the rug beside the bed. Maria was deathly pale, and breathing heavily.

'Go,' he commanded Adele. 'Find Robert and tell him to go at once for Doctor Brent. Tell him to hurry.'

Adele went, running to find her brother deep in great cartons of the embossing paper, which he was unpacking. He turned as she came up, and could see at once that something was amiss.

'Robert. Go for Doctor Brent. Father says he must be fetched at once. Mama is very ill. Go now!'

Within less than an hour the doctor was with them. He stood beside the bed, and turned with an anxious face to William.

'Where is the nurse?' he asked.

'It is her free time,' explained Adele. 'Shall I try to find her?'

Brent shook his head. He had laid his hand upon Mr Moon's hand, and, turning to William he said, 'I'm afraid that no nurse is going to make any difference, sir. Keep as brave a face as you can now. I will stay with you, for I fear that the end is not far off.'

Adele let out a half moan. She and Robert went to stand beside their father at the bedside. William sank to his knees and took his wife's hand in his. They were all silent.

There was a sound on the stairs, and the nurse came in. Doctor Brent gave her a prolonged but quiet look, which she a once understood. She stood beside the doctor. The room was very still. The sound of Maria's breathing had ceased. It was over.

The nurse drew up the sheet, covering Maria's white face. Doctor Brent went round the bed and laid his hand upon William's shoulder. The youngsters clung to each other.

In a very quiet voice, almost a whisper, Doctor Brent said to William, 'Come, sir, let me take you away. We must leave the nurse in attendance.'

William appeared not to hear. He continued to kneel beside his wife until, very gently, Adele and Robert took him by the arms, raised him and drew him from the room.

After his official duties had been dealt with, Doctor Brent joined the family in the sitting room. He shook each of them warmly by the hand and murmured to Adele, 'See to it that your father gets something hot to drink, and take some yourselves. I will come back later this evening.' Saying which, he let himself out.

'Less than twenty five years,' said William to himself.

Adele, returning to the room with cups of hot tea, overheard the words, and it was with deep understanding that she took her father's hand in hers and kissed it.

'Dear Papa,' she said, 'we understand.'

Many people attended the unexpected funeral of Maria Moon. It was a hot day, and the thought occurred to Robert that it might have rained, which would have made matters a great deal worse for everyone.

The Minister took the service, and William himself gave a favourite quotation from the Bible, which he knew by heart. Adele was deeply touched to see him standing here, unable to see anything at all, reciting the words of the Twenty Third Psalm.

That evening, back in the quiet gloom of their home, the three sat silently for some time, until Robert said that he thought they should all retire to bed and try to sleep. They all needed rest.

William went up to the bedroom in which he had spent nights with his wife for many years. How quiet it was, and how empty!

The last few nights had put an almost intolerable strain upon him, yet he had endured them, even slept. But tonight there seemed a finality about his position which tore at his heart. His love for Maria had been deep and constant, and the thought of living without her seemed almost impossible to bear.

All his life, even in times of great stress, William's faith had been such that any grief was never greater than his self control. Now, faced with the prospect of living without Maria, he found that his tears were heavier than his eyelids. They fell, pouring unhindered down his cheeks. William prayed then with an earnestness which he had never felt before. He knew that, deeply emotional as he then was, God's purpose must be fulfilled. When his tears ceased to fall he felt calmer, and finally went to his lonely bed knowing that he must go on with whatever tasks were to be put before him.

Chapter 7

SINCE THE DEATH OF HER MOTHER, Adele had taken charge of much of the running of the house, as well as helping her father at every opportunity.

One afternoon William had gone out on one of his teaching missions and Robert was busy with a translation of one of the foreign alphabets in preparation for printing yet another version of the Lord's Prayer for the missionary societies. Adele had just come into the house from the workshop when there was a ring at the door bell. She went to open the door and was surprised, as well as, she had to admit, pleased to see their young doctor on the doorstep.

'Good afternoon, Miss Moon,' said Doctor Brent. 'I was passing this way and decided that I should look in to see how you all are.'

'That is very kind, Doctor Brent. I'm afraid Papa is out, and Robert is very busy in the workroom. But come in. I'll go and fetch Robert as I know he will be ready for a cup of tea. Would you join us?'

The doctor stepped inside. Adele took his hat and cape, and showed him into the sitting room.

'Do sit down, doctor. If you will excuse me, I will go and put on the kettle and then fetch Robert.'

The doctor sat down and took up a copy of that day's paper. Within a few minutes Adele was back with Robert. After they had all been settled with tea, the doctor spoke about their father.

'How do you think he is, Miss Moon? I have been very concerned about him this past couple of weeks. I thought he looked very strained after your mother's funeral.'

Robert spoke. 'He is still under considerable strain, doctor, but it is only to be expected. He and my mother were very close to each other. We are doing all we can to be of help to him, without, you understand, letting our care be too obtrusive. He is a very self-contained man.'

'That is very considerate, Mr Moon. Your father is one of the most dedicated people that I have ever met. He, I am sure, more than most, appreciates the need to carry on with his great work as normally as possible.'

'He will never let anything at all interfere with the work, no matter how he feels himself,' said Adele. 'We try to go on in as normal a way as we possibly can. We both, Robert and I, keep a careful eye upon Papa, at the same time trying not to let him see it. We are all, of course, under some strain as you will acknowledge, but life must go on. I think the work we have on hand will stand us in good stead. It gives us an anchor.'

After some discussion about things in general, the doctor rose to take his leave. As they shook hands, Robert told him that he was very glad that Doctor Brent had called. 'It was very considerate of you,' he finished.

As she went to the door with the doctor Adele added her own thanks, saying that they would all look forward to seeing him again. The doctor shook hands with her, and the same firm grip gave Adele the feeling of security which she had experienced on an earlier occasion.

Later that evening William came in from his visiting expedition, hung up his coat, and threw himself down in his armchair with an exhausted sigh. Adele looked at him with more than usual attention and was worried to see that he seemed pale and more than usually tired. To cheer him, presently she began to tell him of the visit they had had during the afternoon.

'Doctor Brent is very kind, Papa, and I thought it very agreeable of him to take the trouble to call.'

William listened thoughtfully to his daughter. She, in place of his wife had become a tremendous help, not only in the work, but in the little considerate actions which made him realise afresh how kind and thoughtful she was.

'Did the doctor want anything in particular, my dear?'

'Only to see how we all are, Papa. I thought it extremely civil. He is the easiest of men to get along with, and Robert and I pressed him to come again.'

'I hope he will, then, Adele. I hope also that I might be at home next time he calls.'

'Do you feel that you might make a special date for a visit, Papa?'

'If we can find the time, my love. I think it would be beneficial to have a quiet chat with him one evening.'

'I'll get the calendar, father.' And she went over to the desk in the corner of the room, returning with a diary which seemed to have many items already on its pages.

'We had better consult Robert, too, Papa. In the meantime, whilst you are considering the possibilities, I will go and prepare some supper for you.

I think you need it.' Saying which, she left the room and could be heard moving about in the kitchen.

Adele found herself not a little excited at the thought of spending an evening with their doctor friend.

She was not yet twenty and the thought of meeting with other young people was pleasing. Robert and her father were so tied up with the work: indeed, she herself was becoming much more involved than formerly. Their lives were taken over by the embossing, visiting, and now for her, collecting for the subscriptions as her mother used to do. It was really a hard, extremely busy life, and although she wanted to help her father in every possible way, a little relaxation now and then would be most welcome.

Bringing back the tray with a light meal for her father, Adele found that he had fallen asleep. She laid the tray down on the table beside him very quietly, and tiptoed away. It then occurred to her that perhaps it would have been better if she had not regaled her father with the events of the afternoon. She could have left him to rest quietly, and told him tomorrow. Perhaps she should take more care not to distract him when he came in tired, as he often did. She would bear it in mind.

II

For the next few days Adele kept a careful watch upon her father. He was certainly tired, but appeared to enjoy his work as much as ever. He was deeply involved in his schemes for home teaching as well as visiting those blind people who came to his knowledge. The embossing was taking up every spare moment, and they all had their time filled to capacity. William was naturally of a cheerful nature; his serenity of spirit showing through his every action. Eventually, Adele came to the conclusion that the loss of his wife, added to the daily burden of the work, was responsible for any unusual tiredness which her father might show.

It was, of course, natural that all three of the family would take time to adjust to their recent loss, most of all her father. So, as the embossing work increased and many books were sold, it was found necessary to let the work carry them along, finding fulfilment in any success they might achieve.

It was about a month after Doctor Brent's afternoon visit that time was found for entertaining him one evening. As the day arrived, Adele found herself anticipating it with enjoyment.

The chosen evening was fine, and the doctor walked over to the Moon house in anticipation of what he hoped would be a most pleasant occasion. It was William who let him in, welcoming him with a very warm handshake. They then entered the comfortable sitting room, where Adele and Robert were waiting.

'Ha! This is splendid!' said Doctor Brent. 'I have been looking forward to this evening with the greatest pleasure, I assure you.'

After shaking hands with Robert, the doctor turned to Adele. 'This is a pleasure indeed, Miss Moon. Or may I perhaps call you Miss Adele?'

'Adelaide,' replied Adele a little primly. 'It is only my father and brother who have ever called me Adele. Everyone else knows me as Adelaide.'

'Miss Adelaide, then, if you will permit me,' said the doctor as they all sat down before the evening fire which was welcome in the night air.

'We will sit down to supper almost at once, Doctor,' said William. 'In the meantime, until it is quite ready, perhaps you will be kind enough to tell me how my old friend Doctor Hanson does. It is quite a few months since last I saw him.'

'He does very well, sir.' said Brent. 'The practice seems to grow, however, and he was saying only the other day that he is inclined to appoint another assistant.'

As Adele heard this, she felt a little startled. Did it mean that the family's new friendship with Doctor Brent was to be curtailed almost as soon as it had begun?

Robert intervened. 'I hope that does not mean that we shall be losing you, Doctor Brent?' Thus voicing the innermost thought of Adele.

'Not upon that account, in any case,' was the reply.

Adele excused herself, saying that she would go and bring in the supper, pondering as she did so, why she should so suddenly begin to feel a sense of disappointment.

The meal was well prepared, and William congratulated his daughter upon it. Robert and Brent joined in. Indeed, they were a happy group and enjoyed the food which Adele had prepared, with relish. Afterwards, they again sat around the fire. The conversation then turned towards the effect upon them all of Maria's death.

The doctor asked, in the kindest way, if they were yet feeling more settled. 'If not,' he went on, 'just say the word and I will do anything I can to help.'

William turned the conversation to a more serious note. 'Naturally, we are all having to take time to adjust to our new position, but as we are a Christian family, we find comfort in the knowledge that our dear one is at rest. Also, Doctor, my own feeling is that she is not lost to us. My faith gives me to believe fully in an after life, where we shall meet again in what form is given to us.'

Doctor Brent, although a young man, still in his early thirties, was serious minded, and could appreciate his host's point of view.

'I am of the same opinion, sir,' said Brent. 'Without a sound faith, life would be hard for me, as a doctor. I meet many who begin to despair when faced with illness or death.'

Adele began to feel the atmosphere a little heavy. She loved her father dearly, and had loved her mother to the same degree. However, she was still young and able fully to enjoy pleasant company. She hoped the conversation would take on a lighter vein.

Her father, nevertheless, seemed inclined to continue the discussion. He said, 'Life and death are the two greatest states of our existence here on earth, and beyond. I am of the opinion that we must not live our lives in the belief that death is the end. We must experience death in order to experience the real life which is promised to those who love God and keep His commandments.'

This profundity caused the doctor to pause and think. Adele and Robert had heard their father in this vein many times before. Now they all sat in silence for a few moments.

Then Robert asked Brent if he could tell them more about Doctor Hanson's proposition to appoint another assistant.

'Is the work then so heavy that you are unable to carry it yourself?'

Doctor Brent admitted that upon occasions it was, but then old Doctor Hanson would take a hand. But that, as Adele pointed out, was a burden which Doctor Hanson should not now have to carry.

'He will have to carry more, probably,' said Brent. 'I might as well tell you now that it is likely that I shall not be able to stay here myself, for much longer.'

This was quite a bombshell. They all expected to be able to continue their friendship with Doctor Brent. Adele, in particular, was quite taken aback. So much so, in fact, that she excused herself and said she would go and prepare tea for them.

When she returned with a tray, Robert and Brent stood up to help her. She wondered what conversation she might have missed. When she heard what it had been, she did so with mixed feelings.

Her father spoke. 'I am afraid we might not have the pleasure of entertaining Doctor Brent many more times, my dear,' he told her. 'He tells us that he has an appointment in Australia awaiting him. We shall miss him if he goes, but we would most certainly wish him every success in such a venture, I'm sure.'

'Oh yes, most certainly, Papa,' said Adele, pouring tea, 'but it does seem rather a surprise.'

Doctor Brent told her that he had been offered an appointment as doctor to a vast area in Australia, which would mean much travelling about.

'And would you like to accept it?' asked Robert.

'Yes,'' the doctor said in a serious tone. 'I am happy here, but I feel that there is a great need for any help which can be given out there. I would most certainly like to go.'

'I'm sure the town would miss you, Doctor Brent. We here most certainly would. What does Doctor Hanson think?'

Brent replied that his senior was much of the mind that Australia needed some young blood, and a qualified doctor would be worth his weight in gold to those living in the outback.

'As a matter of fact,' Brent continued, 'Doctor Hanson has been generosity itself to me over this affair. I was of two minds whether to offer my services at all, as I have not been very long here.'

'Such opportunities,' said William, 'are sent to us for a purpose. Sorry though we should be to lose you so soon, it would give us great satisfaction to know that one of your standing, and, if I may say so, sensibilities, should be offering his valuable services out there.'

Robert put in, 'It sounds very attractive to me, Brent. Such an opportunity might never occur again. I could find it in myself to envy you, but my work is here with my father, and there is a very great deal to do.'

'You are right,' answered the doctor. 'I do feel that the opportunity is once for all, and however long I live, I should never get quite such a chance again.'

All this time Adele had been sitting quietly, drinking her tea. When she rose to offer to refill any cups, she spoke to the doctor as she handed him his refilled cup.

'I can only agree with my father and brother. If you do have to leave the town, you will be sorely missed.'

She sat down again, and was quiet and thoughtful for the rest of the evening.

When Doctor Brent finally left, they all shook him warmly by the hand, and he promised, if they were agreeable, to repeat the visit before too long. 'Because,' he said, 'I am not due to leave for another three months, if then.'

The work at the embossing press went on in a very satisfactory manner. William and Robert were kept so busy with their various activities, that their time was filled to the limits, and the pain of losing Maria eased. Adele did as much for her father's work for the blind as she possibly could, and in addition, kept the house and saw to it that her father and brother could always come in to a good meal and a most comfortable home.

They often spoke of Doctor Brent, and Adele found herself thinking of him as she went about her various duties, and wondering whether he had yet made up his mind to go to Australia. She could not deny a feeling of disappointment when she considered the matter. She did not have very long to wait to find the answers to her queries on the subject. As she passed the window one day, she saw a figure outside apparently coming up to the front door. The bell rang, and Adele went to open the door. The visitor was Doctor Brent. A feeling of pleasurable excitement mounted in Adele's thoughts. The doctor entered and she took him to the sitting room.

'This is an unexpected pleasure, Doctor,' she said. 'Is there anything we can do for you?'

The doctor stood up and took a turn about the room. When he spoke, he went to stand nearer to Adele.

'Miss Moon, or shall I say Miss Adelaide?'

Adele laughed. 'I am quite happy with either,' she said.

'I want to talk to you about a very serious matter which affects me deeply,' said Brent.

'And what might that be?' Adele smiled, but she began to feel uncertain of what might follow.

'I have decided that I must go to Australia, but before I can make definite and final plans, there is something which I must ask you.'

'Ask me?' queried Adele. 'I will help in any way I can, but would you not rather talk to Father, or Robert? If it is a very important matter concerning your trip, I might not be the best person to offer advice or help.'

'It is certainly about my trip, and until I have spoken to you, yourself, about my plans, I would not wish to talk either to your brother or your father.'

A certain tension was mounting in Adele. She could not, dared not, anticipate the doctor's question. He the said,

'Adelaide, what I must know is this. Would you be willing to consider coming out to Australia with me?'

Adele gasped. In her heart she knew that she would gladly take the risk of travelling across the world to be able to help this young doctor. There was a pause before the doctor spoke again.

'I would consider it a great honour to have you out there with me, as my wife.'

He let this statement hang in the air, saying no more, and waiting for Adele's reaction. A thousand reasons why she could not go out there with him came to her mind. She found herself trembling. Doctor Brent looked so very earnest. Presently she found her voice.

'You have done me the greatest honour, Doctor Brent. But you must realise that I need time to think. I cannot decide upon so important an issue on the spur of the moment.'

'That is very understandable,' said Brent. 'I have said nothing at all to anyone else, as I thought that you must be the first recipient of my desires. Can you give me any encouraging answer at all, do you think?'

'I'm afraid I cannot, Doctor. It is a matter of deep concern, needing prayer. I also feel that I should discuss it with Papa. Would that be acceptable?'

'I should be glad for you to have the opportunity, Adele, if I may venture your pet name. If you are willing, I will come back again at the end of the week, and hear what your decision is.'

Adele saw him out and, returning in a state of indecision she went up to her room and sat quietly, trying to take in what had just occurred. Of course, she told herself, she could never consider leaving her father. He needed her as he had never needed her before. The work for the blind was of such great moment to him, and to Robert and even to herself.

She came to the conclusion that she must retire early that night, and spend some time with her Bible, and in prayer. The habit in the Moon household was always to lay every important consideration before God, confident that whatever the outcome, it would be the right one.

She decided to say nothing to her father or Robert at this point. Her decisions, she felt, must be her own, and come from the heart. Therefore, as they retired for the night, she closed her bedroom door on every other consideration and sat down with her Bible where she was sure she would find guidance. It was well over an hour before she was ready to seek her bed. Her mind was made up: she would say nothing to her father until she had seen Brent again. Eventually, she slept, but it was a rather uneasy sleep. When she woke, she offered another prayer for help, and began on the day's work.

William had asked Adele the previous day, if she would be able to do some collecting for the next subscription which was now due. There were several promised amounts to be gathered in, and Adele had undertaken to do it. She was glad of the excuse to be out of the house for an hour or two, and, while walking around, had given further deep thought to her present problem. Before the task was completed and Adele nearly home again, she had decided that she must, after all, talk to her father, and soon. She needed to know what her father's reaction would be.

That evening she would have the opportunity of talking to her father alone, since Robert was to be out giving a talk at their local chapel. After supper was cleared away, she approached her father who was sitting busily at his desk, writing letters, which was always a difficult problem when he had to write them himself.

'Papa, are you so very busy?'

'Yes, as a matter of fact, I am. There are at least half a dozen letters which I must write. Why, what makes you ask?'

'I want to talk to you, Papa, on a very important matter.'

'Why, Adele, my dear, what is it? I hope you are not worried about something.'

'Not worried, exactly, but I would like to talk to you about it rather specially.'

'Very well, my dear. I will just finish this letter, and then I'll put them away for an hour, and we'll talk.'

'Rather mystified, William drew up his armchair, and sat waiting for Adele to speak.

'Father, I want to tell you this as gently as I can. You will be very surprised, I think.'

'If I were not before, I am now waiting with bated breath to hear what you have to tell me.'

'Yesterday, Papa, Doctor Brent called while you and Robert were working. Although he has not yet broached the subject to you, he wants me to go out to Australia with him, as his wife.'

William listened intently to Adele. He had to admit that upon the few occasions when he had heard Brent in Adele's company, and had thought there might be a friendship there, he was now quite taken aback. He was silent for a moment or two, then he said, 'And what do you say to such a proposal, my dear?'

It was typical of William that he would never impose his own thoughts upon anyone who was appealing to him. He would always listen carefully to the other person's viewpoint, and only after that, when specifically asked, state what his reaction was.

'Papa, I could never leave you, especially at this time. I thought long and hard yesterday about it, and that is my conclusion.'

William was silent, considering carefully what he must do. Eventually he said to Adele, 'And do you love this young man?'

'I thought perhaps I did,' replied Adele. 'I have been very happy in his company and we seem to think along similar lines. But now, when I consider it, I find that even with him, I could not face being at such a distance from you and Robert. Then of course, there is your work here, and I want to help with that in every way that I can.'

'I respect your decision, my love, but I must ask you to be quite certain that you would not be unhappy if he were to go away, no doubt for life, so that you would not meet again. I appreciate your desire to help me and, indeed, you have been my inspiration for a long time. But I could not agree to standing in your way if you really felt you must go.'

There was silence again, which neither felt prepared to break. Adele thought of the young doctor, so pleasant, so helpful and considerate, and in whose company she felt secure. William, on the other hand, felt that his daughter's feelings were being honestly expressed. She appeared to have no deep distress and was quite calm.

'My love,' William said at last, 'although I could be upset at the thought that Brent approached you before speaking to me, I understand his predicament, and fully appreciate that he would not be willing to co-erce you in any way. I know he would have come openly and honestly to me if your decision had been to go with him. To tell the truth, Adele, I feel pity for him. I trust that when he goes he will find compensation in his work and a complete fulfilment in it.'

'Thank you, Papa. I knew I should be doing the right thing in coming to such a decision as I have. I could really not bear to be on the other side of the world, and unable to work with you and Robert.'

Father and daughter sat in complete understanding with each other, in a companiable silence for a further few minutes. Then Adele asked whether her father thought she should write to Doctor Brent, or should they ask him to come and see them.

'He did say that he would like to come, Papa, when I had had time to think. I think I would prefer that, as then I could be sure how he feels about my decision, and we can both give him our warm good wishes for his success out there.'

'I think that is right, Adele. We will look into the possible times when we could invite him. I have to go close to the surgery tomorrow, and I could drop in a letter telling him what we suggest.'

'Thank you, dear Papa,' cried Adele, throwing her arms about him, and kissing him. 'I feel quite settled now in my mind, and quite convinced that what I am doing is the right thing.'

So it was that towards the end of the week, Doctor Brent again found himself sitting with the Moon family. Adele had taken him aside and told him her decision. She knew that his disappointment was great, but she knew also that his considerate nature would appreciate her position.

They had a pleasant talk for over an hour, and then the doctor left, shaking hands most warmly with them all, pressing Adele's hand in a close grasp.

'God go with you, my boy,' said William, and was pleased to hear there was no downcast tone in his young friend's voice.

A few years later they were happy to have news of the success of the doctor's venture. He was highly esteemed by all who knew him. But he did not marry.

Chapter 8

WILLIAM'S FAME WAS SPREADING. Already he had been honoured as a Fellow of the Royal Geographical Society and of the Royal Society of Arts. More honours were to be bestowed upon him as the years went by, but, as he himself always said when any satisfactory conclusion to a project had been reached: to God be the glory. His modesty was absolute, and in his quiet, natural way, he worked away with one object always, and only, in his mind. Let the blind see the light: enable them to read. This, from the early days of his complete blindness had been foremost in his mind and heart. He maintained, from those early days until he could work no more, that his blindness had been given him as a talent. It was, as he had said, an apprenticeship which must be worked at in order to do what he was convinced was God's special intention for him.

In spite of his serious intent, William was a very happy, cheerful person whom it was good to be with. Many people had occasion to thank him for advice, help, and encouragement. He never spared himself.

William and his son worked prodigiously on the Moon theme. Robert spent many weeks working on the translations of foreign languages in order to fit them to the Moon system.

Missionaries in all parts of the world were thankful to the Moon family for their selfless efforts on behalf of blind people whom they could never hope to meet.

William now had another idea. Travelling about, visiting so many who had been born blind, he was sensitive to their needs. Any blind from birth would have no visual image of what was about them, and this, William found deeply distressing. He began to have pictures embossed: people, buildings, animals, trees, and anything which he felt would enable them to learn shapes of the things they heard talked of. William himself felt that he was fortunate in that he could remember things seen in his childhood and youth. His incentive to bring such knowledge to all blind people with whom he came into contact, was great. Among the variety of embossed pictures he included some of the Queen and Buckingham Palace. Other buildings of national interest were also included, and his embossed pictures gave infinite comfort to many. It was Robert who made himself responsible for making the original drawings ready for embossing, in the same way that he had also undertaken the work of preparing foreign alphabets. The latter were used by missionaries all over the world, making them able to teach their blind to read the embossed portions of Scripture, the Lord's Prayer, and other uplifting literature.

Adele was as busy as her father and brother, and unstinting in her efforts to further their great projects. She found her time most fully occupied and it was now only occasionally that she spared thought for their distant friend, Doctor Brent. She hoped that all was well with him, remembering him with an affectionate kindness. Nevertheless, she was now quite certain that her decision regarding him had been the right one. She was happy, working with Robert and her father; running the home, and bringing cheerful comfort to her menfolk so that they might come in from the workshop and relax.

They were a happy trio, made all the happier by the great satisfaction that their work gave them all.

One Sunday, after morning service in their nonconformist church, one of the elders remarked to William that it seemed a pity that they should have to break up so soon in the day. An afternoon meeting was suggested.

'What sort of meeting could be undertaken?' asked William.

Adele broke in, 'I think it would be splendid if you were to start a Sunday meeting, Father.'

'I? What should I speak about?'

The elder remarked that William had plenty to speak about. 'Many, many people, William, are more than interested in your work for the blind, to start with. Then, of course, it would give you an opportunity to do a little preaching. You are adept at that, and it would help to fill the gap which I know you feel in not having entered the Ministry yourself.'

'You are very kind, and very persuasive, George,' said William. 'Has anyone else spoken of such a meeting?'

'As a matter of fact,' said George, a tubby little man with a kindly smile, 'one or two of the other elders in our group have expressed a wish that we might have a Sunday afternoon meeting.'

As William said, there would be a great deal to discuss about such a project. First of all, where could it be held? As they parted company William promised to hold it in mind.

The following Sunday a good deal more was said about the suggestion of a Sunday meeting. After church, the other elders and one or two interested members of the congregation gathered in the vestibule. Several opinions were expressed, not the least of which was the idea that William should undertake to hold a Sunday afternoon meeting, regularly. They said that he would have their full support.

One of the elders was a town councillor who volunteered the information that the Town Hall was not used much on a Sunday, and that room could be made there if only William would promise to speak.

'Your work for the blind would fill the hall any time,' said one.

William was thoughtful. He began to envisage many blind, whom he knew well, apart from sighted people, attending a gathering such as was being put forward. He promised to give it his consideration. That night, of course, he held it in his prayers.

So it was that the Sunday afternoon meetings which William addressed were started. They were to continue for many years and William never regretted his decision. The meeting became very popular and was always well attended. It filled a gap in the lives of many people, particularly those blind who had received so much help from William over the years. William's deep faith, as well as his joy in the Scriptures, came over in full measure to his audience.

During the nineteenth century the Bible was read in nearly every home, and to those who could not read it for themselves the comfort it gave was the greater. William's Sunday Afternoons became an institution not to be missed.

II

William was now busier than ever. The embossing work was well in hand and the two or three workmen kept the press in constant use. Books were in great demand as were always the pictures, and the sales began to rise. Orders were received from near and far, and the Moon system began to be known all over the world.

As William was so busy he had no time for indulging (as he put it) in sadness or depression. He still missed his wife daily, but, even so, he found that his constant activity kept him alive. The Stimulus of the Sunday afternoon meetings gave an added fillip to life. He was well content.

His more recent idea to provide embossed pictures for the blind was most satisfactory. Those who had been born blind had no idea what the world and its inhabitants looked like. Animals, to them, were just the name of a noise they might hear, such as the barking of a dog, the low of cattle, the crow of a cockerel. This state of affairs needed immediate attention.

William talked to Robert about this, and it was Robert who undertook to draw the pictures ready for embossing. Music was embossed, and hymns written in Moon. Even the stars were not forgotten, and the embossed pictures of all these were very popular indeed.

Not only were hymns, music, stars and so on made available to the blind, but Euclid was introduced in the publications.

As the year wore on, and Christmas drew near, it was decided that they would call a halt for a couple of days, and relax. Christmas Day itself saw a crisp, cold morning, so that they set out for the service in their chapel in a bouyant mood. Back home, Robert saw to it that there was a good fire round which they would sit, enjoying each other's company in a quiet way. This was an unusual treat for the three of them, since their time was always taken up with the activities of their calling.

The room was of a good size and, being on the first floor of the house it was always relatively warm. Today it was Robert's job to keep a cheerful fire, and he hauled up a basket of logs from the workroom downstairs in order, as his father said, to eke out the coal. They had never been in the least degree wealthy, but certainly living was now a good deal easier than it had ever been in William's and Maria's early married life. As Robert threw on a fresh log, making the sparks fly, it was on this topic that William began to reminisce.

'I shall never forget the time when you were born, Adelaide.'

At this remark, Adele looked up sharply. Her father never called her by her full name in the family circle. Her pet name of Adele was the usual form of address between them. William noticed the sudden movement, and smiled warmly in her direction.

'Yes, Adele,' he went on, 'it was a most trying time. We were almost penniless, and I had to carry out all the household chores, and attend to you two, and your mother, as well as going to school all day.'

'But it was worth it, father, wasn't it?' asked Robert with a grin. Adele saw his expression and smiled at him in response.

'Oh yes, having both of you was well worth all the effort it entailed. I only wish, as I know your mother did, that we had had more of the necessities of life at that time. It seems,' he went on, 'a long time since your mother was with us, and it would make me very happy to see her sitting here with us now.'

There was a short silence which Adele broke.

'I do so agree with you, Papa, and so, I'm sure, does Robert. We all miss her, but you, Papa, of all people, must believe that she is safe in other hands now.'

William sighed but he agreed with his daughter, and admitted it. 'I know we shall always miss her, but, as you say, we must be grateful that she is in better hands than ours.'

Another pause followed, then Robert put his foot to the log which had slipped slightly and was in danger of falling out of the grate. He was a handsome young man, as near a replica of his father as it was possible to be. Dark hair and eyes and now, a moustache. He and William made a striking pair.

As the silence continued, William was feeling how happy it would make him, to be able to see his son and daughter sitting there. In spite of the fact that he was determined to live a busy, full life without Maria, and was partially succeeding, there were many times when, in his secret heart, he found himself wishing that his wife was there with him, to tell him those things which most parents enjoy together: the sight of the youngsters, how they looked, what they were about and all the little intimate things about them. Although William's grief at the loss of Maria was greater than any other he had ever felt, even at the time of his becoming totally blind, he was overcoming it and finding many happy moments in his life to enjoy. He brought his thoughts back to the present.

'We must not let Christmas be a sad occasion,' he said. 'We understand each other, and it is quite right and proper to fill our lives as much as we can with happier things.'

Adele rose. 'Quite right, Papa dear. Mama would not wish us to sit in miserable silence today of all days.'

'So, Adele,' put in Robert, 'I propose that you now go and make us a cup of tea, and we enjoy the rest of this day cheerfully.'

'I have a better idea, brother,' retorted Adele, laughing. 'You go and make the tea. It will be a change for you.'

Robert rose, passing his sister with a light tap on her head. He went out, grinning, and presently returned with a loaded tray which he triumphantly placed on the table beside his father's chair.

'Well done, Robert,' laughed Adele. 'Let's see if you've put any tea in the pot. Robert has made the tea, Papa, so we'll see what it's like!'

As they sat, relaxed, sipping the tea which, Adele had to admit, was perfect, there was a contentment in the room.

'It's good to see you resting, Father,' remarked Robert presently. 'It seems a very rare occurrence these days.'

'There's nothing like work, my boy, especially if it is the sort of work you enjoy, and I certainly enjoy mine. I must admit that now and then I get upset when I meet one of the poorer uneducated blind. It gives me great comfort, nevertheless, when I can give them a few verses from the Scriptures, and watch them managing to read it.'

'We shall probably see a few of them tomorrow, Papa,' said Adele, 'when we go to the tea party in the church rooms. I happen to know that a number of them are looking forward to it with tremendous pleasure. It's all your doing, you know.'

'That it is not,' retorted William vehemently. 'We now have several willing workers visiting these people.'

'I know that,' said Adele, 'but it all began with your dedication. Isn't that so, Robert?' she finished, turning to her brother.

'Of course. Papa must know it too, but he is too modest to admit it.' Then, turning to his father again, he went on, 'Do you remember that poor old man in the blind hospital in Holland? I'll never forget the joy on his face when he found that someone cared about him.'

'Yes, I recall him,' said William, 'but there were many people trying to help, and they also cared.'

'Well,' said Adele, 'we know the hours you have laboured and the effort you have put in; are still putting in as well.'

'That's enough about me,' said William, mildly rebuking his children. 'It pleases me enormously that both of you are now also involved. What I would do without your help, I tremble to think.'

To change the subject, Adele got up and poured another cup of tea for her father. Robert, too, felt the need for a little lighter topic and, as his sister passed him also another cup of tea, he remarked gaily to her, 'I say, Adele. You are looking particularly becoming this afternoon.' Turning to his father, he described what Adele was wearing. 'She's in a long, purple (I think) skirt, Papa, an has a most elegant white blouse on.'

'Thank you, brother,' said Adele, smiling. 'Such a remark from you is praise indeed. But don't run away with the idea that I have been extravagant, Papa. I made these things during the Autumn and I feel rather pleased with the result. I chose the purple, Father, as a change from the black I have been wearing. I hope you don't object.'

'Why should I object, my dear? I am sure that if I could see you, I should be even more pleased than I am, to hear how industrious you have been, and to hear Robert's praise.'

After a few moments silence, Robert returned to the subject of their visits to Holland. He told how excited they were when they took the press to Holland and William's very first piece of embossed type was written on the very night of the day they sailed.

'Yes, that was certainly a red letter day, wasn't it? Although it is a few years ago, I can still feel the joy of those people when they realised what benefit was to be theirs. It was certainly a day to remember.'

'I wish I could have gone,' said Adele, a little wistfully.

'But you were only a schoolgirl, my love. Besides, you had to keep Mama company. No doubt the time will come when you will be able to go with me on a journey,' said William.

'I shall look forward to that, Papa. The only thing is that, if I went as well as you, and Robert was as busy as ever, who would keep house?'

'I find,' said William, 'that occasions provide their own arrangements. I am quite satisfied to go from day to day, carrying on with our work, and not worrying one bit about any future plans. Is there any more tea?'

And so the day wore on and they spent the evening content with each other's company, remembering the past and putting their faith in the future.

Chapter 9

THE NEXT YEAR PROVED TO BE another very busy one for William. Travelling, with Robert as escort and helper, on the new railway systems, he visited a number of his Home Teaching Societies. He was delighted to visit again his friend, Sir Charles Lowther, who had been so generous both with donations in money and gifts of numbers of books. Blind himself, Sir Charles had every sympathy for those other blind, less fortunate people whom William was able to help.

The two friends talked long into the night, leaving Robert to browse through the extensive library which the house contained. William reminded Charles of that great occasion when he, Charles, had made that generous donation which enabled them to extend the Moon premises and workshops.

'I have been more than fortunate,' said William. 'I have, and am still, receiving such tremendous support from all over the country, even over the world, and I find it difficult to believe that such benefits should come my way.'

'Nonsense,' replied his friend. 'Why, even the Queen herself has commended you, and expressed the greatest admiration for all you are doing.'

'She has certainly been very gracious,' agreed William, 'and I am most indebted to Her Majesty. I am, also, greatly indebted to the missionary societies up and down the world and such bodies as the British and Foreign Bible Society, all of whom have given me the most generous support, allowing my system to be translated into so many languages. I am a most fortunate man.'

They parted for the night, and Robert took his father up to his bedroom and saw him into bed. The next morning they were up early, and on their travels once more, this time visiting some of the nearer societies in the greater comfort of Sir Charles's carriage which he put at their disposal for the rest of the day. Robert could see that his father was touched by the kindness he always received but silently he could not really wonder at it. His admiration for his father was great, and he felt that whatever he could find to do for him would be most gladly carried out.

That had always been Robert's attitude and it was obvious, also, that Adele was of the same mind. Between them, they were to give yeoman service to their father throughout his life, and as it was to be proved, they would carry on beyond that time.

As they travelled about the Northern Counties together, Robert often looked at his father with admiration and a deep love. This man to whom he owed his existence was one of the world's saints. Always cheerful, deeply religious, thoroughly Christian in his attitude to others, and still, as always, determined to give all he could to those who suffered from his own disability.

There present plans took them to a number of Home Teaching groups, and into the homes of many who were full of thankfulness and praise for William Moon and his ability to bring reading sight to the blind.

The next few years were productive ones. The work load increased, and the premises were extended. Whenever William returned from visiting, he always found himself loaded with orders for more books, pamphlets and pictures. On the present occasion, when he and Robert returned from their visit to the Northern Home Teaching Societies, the order book was filled almost to overflowing. But not only were they kept more than busy, there were other considerations and events to be met.

It was nearly two years since William's wife had died. He was still a comparatively young man. He had married very young, and they had had only a little over twenty years together. He was not yet fifty.

Back home, William decided to visit one or two of his local groups. He was interested to find that there was a new helper in the field. She was full of energy, very kind, and vigorous in her efforts to further the work. She was in charge of one of the groups which William then visited, and welcomed him warmly. They were meeting in her father's house, and William was grateful to find how sympathetic they were towards him and his various projects. When he was back home he found himself telling Adele about these new helpers.

'You seem very impressed, Papa,' said Adele.

'To be truthful, I am,' answered her father. 'I am always surprised when I find new helpers in the field.'

'I think perhaps people are more impressed with what you have achieved than you know. Whenever I visit any of these groups, I am always received with open arms. People on the whole are kind, and well disposed towards such needs as you have made public.'

William thought about his daughter. She was surprising him by the intensity of her feelings. Yet why should he be so surprised. She was her mother's daughter, and no-one could have given him more support than Maria had. The same applied to Robert, of course. He was extremely fortunate in having two such staunch helpers.

No more was said that evening on the subject of the new workers in his cause, but William found himself thinking about them rather more than he usually did about those concerned people he so often met with. He had a very great deal to be thankful for. Everything, in fact, he told himself, as he remembered the day's events in his prayers that night.

II

The summer drew on and gave way to Autumn. William's sister, Jane, had for some years being living abroad as companion to the elderly lady in whose employ she had spent many years. After the old lady had died, Jane had stayed in Italy where she had made a home for herself, but now she felt the urge to visit her brother and make the acquaintance of her niece and nephew. She therefore sold her house in Italy, had her belongings stored in England, and travelled back to find somewhere to live.

As Jane was now in her sixties, the urge for the companionship of a family of her own was very great. Eventually, she arrived in England, and made haste to contact William. Her brother was delighted to have Jane back home, and it was with great interest and satisfaction that he learned that she was to build a home only a few miles from where William and his family were living. It was a splendid arrangement, and from then on, Jane was able to enjoy the family contacts which she had so sorely missed.

The work load at the press grew heavier; the output was prodigious. William was finding that embossed material was being called for from all parts of the world. He found it difficult to believe that his simple system, invented as it was, in order to help mainly the blind children with whom he first made contact, was becoming so successful and such a blessing to so many hundreds of people. As always, he praised God and thanked Him daily for crowning his, William's, endeavours.

An even greater satisfaction was to be his. One day, as he was helping in the workshop, Adele came excitedly to him.

'Papa, what do you think?'

'You seem very pleased about something, by the sound of it,' he answered. 'What is it?'

'The post has just brought a letter from Australia, Papa. It is from Doctor Brent.'

William hesitated before making further comment. It occurred to him that perhaps, after all, his daughter regretted her decision not to go to Australia with Brent. He waited for her to continue.

'Oh Papa, it is very good news. He has been in contact with some blind people in his area, and, what do you think? They are all learning to read from your system!'

'That is wonderful news, indeed, my love,' said William. Then he hesitated before saying, 'And what else does Brent say?'

'That he is well and very happy, and extremely busy with patients over a vast area. He says he is delighted to be able to report about the blind one, and that he has been very proud to let them know that he knows the man who invented their embossed books.'

'That is all very gratifying, my dear. It certainly sounds as though he has found the right niche for himself. Shall you reply to the letter?'

'Yes, Papa, I will, and I shall tell him how pleased we all are at his news. I'll ask Robert to write a word as well. I expect the doctor will appreciate a letter from the family.'

And that was all. William felt a sense of relief that his daughter seemed quite content at home. He had several times wondered whether she was as happy and contented as she appeared. Now he knew, and was grateful for it. Other thoughts came to him about Adele. Was she really contented to run their home? Feelings were stirring in William's heart and mind which he had not expected, nor experienced for some years.

Some time later William found himself in the company of that lady who had, within the past few months, made such great contributions to the visiting programme in the locality. He had gone to call on one particular family in whom he was more than usually interested, as there were two generations of blind in the house. He liked to find out for himself what progress was being made with the older brother helping his young sister to read from the embossed type. They were very pleased to welcome William, as always, and happy to tell him that Miss Anne was there. 'Miss Anne' was the pet name with which many of the local blind knew the visitor, and wherever she went there seemed to be laughter. It was so on this occasion, and William was glad to join in with any fun which might be going. The visit was a happy one, and, when he was due to leave, William found that he was very pleased to have the company of 'Miss Anne' for the rest of the afternoon.

Miss Anne reported to William on the results of the several visits she had made, not only to that particular family, but to many others as well. She expressed the wish that she would be glad of any advice which Mr Moon might be able to give her, as, of course, he had known the local people for so much longer than she had.

'We are having a meeting of a few local helpers at my home next

Tuesday,' he told Miss Anne. 'I wonder whether you would care to join us? My son and daughter will be there of course, and one or two of those whom you have already met.'

'That sounds very pleasant, Mr Moon,' said Miss Anne. 'I would like, very much, to be able to come and talk with you all, to find out if there are any other ways in which we might help these unfortunate people. What time will you be holding the meeting?'

'At half past seven. It will give me great pleasure to have you with us, and I shall look forward to sharing our experiences.'

As they parted, William shook hands warmly with his friend, and, familiar as he was with the way home, returned happily and with a sense of expectation.

The week-end followed its usual course of activity. The Sunday meetings, first of all at church in the morning, and then at the Town Hall in the afternoon, kept them all busy. Their usual evening Bible reading which was a regular Sunday event, rounded the day with a sense of quiet achievement. Monday was, as usual, crowded with the activities of the workshop, and, as Tuesday dawned, William found himself making careful plans with Adele and Robert about the forthcoming meeting that evening.

The meeting went well. Discussions were lively, and each one felt that encouragement had been received from the interchange of experiences and ideas. Adele and Robert had met all the others face to face, and it occurred to Robert, as it so often did, that his father was at a disadvantage in not seeing the friends he knew so well. Yet his father never showed any sense of resentment or dissatisfaction. He was always his cheerful, courteous self, giving out so much in support to all those who worked with him and for him.

As the meeting broke up, William made a point of asking Miss Anne whether she felt that the meeting had been worth while. She replied that most certainly it had, and that, if Mr Moon would care to invite her again, she would look forward to another such evening with the greatest enjoyment.

As the door was closed and locked for the night behind the last visitor, Robert said to his father, 'What a happy group they are, Father, especially Miss Anne. She is one of the kindest people I think I have ever met.'

William agreed. 'I wonder whether Adele feels the same?'

But Adele had gone up to her room and retired for the night, so no opinion was given.

When William himself retired he found himself considering what the reactions of his children would be if he continued the train of thought which seemed to recur with regularity.

Christmas was again approaching and plans had to be made to fit in extra visits to the local groups. The work load was higher than it had ever been. Orders for books came in daily and the embossing was at fever pitch. One evening after a particularly hectic day, as they sat at supper, William decided that he must seek the opinions of Robert and Adele about his future plans. They were all three tired, and after finishing the meal, they took seats round the fire and rested.

Presently, William spoke. 'Has either of you any special item to be considered for our Christmas meetings?'

Robert spoke first. 'I was wondering, Father, whether we could get that little group of helpers together again, and ask them to take on the extra visiting during Christmas time?'

'That seems to me to be a sound plan, Robert,' replied his father. 'We shall have to draw up a programme so that no family is omitted, and everyone gets a significant visit.'

'We must also think of all our extra work, Papa,' put in Adele. 'I find myself rushing down to the workshop in the midst of preparing meals.'

'Could you do with some help, then, Adele?'

'Most certainly I could. Only the other day I found I had to leave the workshop and run upstairs at speed in order to save our dinner. You and Robert might just as well have come up to a piece of dry bread. But more help would cost more money, Father.'

William was silent for a few moments, then he said: 'Would it be acceptable to you, Adele, if someone came in to do all the housekeeping for you, and left you free to carry out what I consider to be very valuable work with the books?'

Robert glanced from his father to his sister and back again. An intrusive thought had just occurred to him, but he found it well nigh impossible to accept it. He said, 'Have you any plan especially in mind, Father?'

Adele also looked up sharply. 'If you are thinking that we should employ a housekeeper, Papa, I must say that, although it would be good to be free to help in your work, we just could not afford to pay such a person a reasonable salary.'

William was in a quandary. He could hardly credit the way his thoughts were actually going. Should he openly admit to them what had been happening in his mind these three months or more? Would Adele feel put out of countenance? Would she resent another female in their compact and happy household? What would Robert's reactions be if he found himself with a step mother? But William knew he had to open his heart to them. He had, as he always had, prayed about the situation in which he now found himself. He must take the plunge.

'I do not know whether you feel that this moment is the proper one for what I wish to say to you both.'

Adele and Robert looked at each other, wondering whatever was coming.

William went on... 'I must be open and honest with you, my dears. What would your reactions be if I were to marry again?'

The ejaculation was mutual. Robert and Adele each cried: 'Father!'

'I feared it might come as a shock to you both, but you must know that I do feel the need of a consort. I have missed your mother sorely, particularly when it has been necessary for me to attend certain functions and meetings alone because both of you are busy with your projects.'

A flash of insight illumined Adele's brain. 'Papa, I have just received the conviction that you are referring to Miss Anne. Am I right?'

Robert shifted in his chair. The evening had been a chilly one, and he had taken on his usual task of tending the fire. He threw on more coal.

William was relieved to realise that Adele had happened to hit on the one person who was constantly in his thoughts. He waited for further reactions from either or both of them.

'You are quite right, my love,' he said to Adele. 'I find myself completely at one with Miss Anne, and I venture to think that she feels at home with me. I have talked with her on a great many occasions during our visits, and she has been of the utmost help and comfort to me.' He paused. Then... 'Would you be willing for me to take this step, and would you, also, like to think about it for a day or two and let me know your decisions?'

'Father,' said Robert, 'If your peace of mind and happiness rely upon your taking this step, you must take it. I, for one, would be so pleased to feel that there was someone to whom you could turn and who would take care of you in many ways. I don't know what Adele feels...'

Adele sat with folded hands. She was quietly looking into the fire and considering what it might be like to have another woman in the home, taking her place. The place which she had so aptly fulfilled since the death of her mother a couple of years before.

She said, 'My first reaction seems to be one of gratitude to think that there might be someone willing to care for you as a wife would. But I would like, if you don't mind, Papa, to have time to consider my own feelings and to try to face up to what it might mean for me. Is that selfish?'

'Selfish! Of course not. Take all the time you need. We will leave the matter tonight, and when we are home in the evening again on Saturday, perhaps we can discuss it again. In the meantime, I will say nothing to Anne.'

They both noticed the 'Anne'. It seemed to confirm their joint feelings.

The next day or two seemed to fly past with no time to think about much else but the embossing and printing, making timetables for the Christmas visitings, and generally keeping up as well as they might with the work load.

On the Saturday morning as she prepared the meals for the week-end, Adele found herself thinking rather enviously of how much easier it might be to have none of this to worry about. Her mind was preoccupied with the cataloguing and packing of the books which were being produced at such a vast rate. Perhaps she would rather be free to devote her time to the workshop and the other activities which she undertook on her father's behalf. Robert, she felt, would not be affected in quite the same way as she would, if their father re-married. He had very few commitments in the kitchen, for instance, and apart from seeing to the fires in Winter, he had very little responsibility in the home. She, on the other hand, was constantly at the beck and call of her menfolk, of mealtimes, of shopping which had to be done occasionally if they were to be fed. She felt herself to be of a slightly more academic frame of mind than domesticated. Yet she had always enjoyed being in charge of the house and taking her mother's place.

Nevertheless, she told herself, her father's wishes must come first. She loved him dearly, and as so often in her thinking, she considered his great handicap. To someone completely blind, surely every consideration for their comfort must be given. She had made up her mind.

Robert came up from the workshop and, finding his sister standing in the middle of the kitchen with a wooden spoon in one hand and a copper kettle in the other, he teased her. 'What on earth are you doing, Adele? You seem to be dreaming, and want to be careful of that kettle. Either fill it, or empty it, whichever you are supposed to be doing. It's heavy, anyway.'

'I was thinking about Father,' said Adele. 'Have you come to any decision yet as to what you would like him to do?'

'As a matter of fact, I have,' answered Robert. 'Have you?'

Adele nodded. She told him that she would not be happy if she stood in the way of what her father wanted, even needed. She would like to be able to devote all her time to the embossing, and record making, and so on. She felt that her work in that direction really meant more to her than anything else.

She was still holding the kettle in one hand. Robert went towards her and relieved her of it. 'Let's put this thing away, Adele. The next thing will be we shall have water all over the floor.' Then, turning to his sister, he said, 'So your mind is made up? So is mine. If that is what Father wants, that is what he must have. I like Anne and I have seen her with Father on visits and at meetings, and it seems to me that she is just the right person to have about him.'

That evening, seated round the fire again, supper cleared away, and a warm, relaxed atmosphere in the room, Robert spoke to his father in a kind, but serious manner.

'Father, we have both given much thought to what we were discussing the other evening. We want you to be happy, and we are both more than agreeable to your marrying Anne. We both like her very much, and no doubt we shall all get on extremely well together.'

William found the wind rather taken out of his sails.

'Bless you both, my dear children. You have put my mind at ease. Now let us talk about whatever plans we must make for the Christmas meetings. I will see Anne tomorrow at Church, and would like to invite her to dinner if Adele is willing.'

Adele got up, went across to her father and ruffled his hair. 'Dear Papa,' she said, 'you know we love you, and if Anne is willing to do the same, let's make her welcome.'

There was no need for further discussion about this so vital and important matter. They were all of one mind and they all looked forward to tomorrow's dinner with keen expectation.

Chapter 10

THE NEXT TWO OR THREE MONTHS saw a gradual change in the Moon household. Anne was a constant visitor and had already, before her marriage, begun to lend a hand whenever she could. Adele was finding her a delightful companion and looked forward with keen interest to the days when she would be with them completely.

It was two or three months later when arrangements were finalised and the marriage took place. The day was bright and clear and the general atmosphere in the Moon household was one of happiness. It augured well for their combined futures. William and Anne spent a few days away and, returning to find Adele and Robert in the midst of a heavy demand for books. At once, Anne threw herself into the fray, and the extra help on such a permanent basis was extremely valuable.

Anne came to be known affectionately as Annie. She took over the complete running of the domestic affairs from Adele, leaving her free to join forces with Robert and her father. There was only one aspect of his work that William found still to be irksome. A secretary was needed.

William's correspondence grew apace. Robert still had to supervise the embossing of all salient points in the letters, but even with any assistance which Annie had time to give him, he found the task of keeping up to date with them almost impossible. After some discussion it was decided that a secretary was essential. Subscriptions were still coming in, and, with their help it was found that the post of secretary could now be filled.

The young woman who took on this position proved to be worth her weight in gold. Not only did she deal with all William's correspondence, but she found time to help in the workshop and could often be found assembling pages of Moon type, or packing up parcels of books to be sent away. Altogether, she and the family became a splendid team. Even the youngest assistant in the workshop found himself to be a contented team member. The work, therefore, still grew and the output was colossal.

The next ten years found the total output to be in the region of thirty thousand plates. William Moon's modest but determined efforts to bring sight to the blind when he was a young man of about twenty two, had brought reading to thousands throughout the world.

A further triumph of achievement was to be the amazing number and variety of alphabets in little known foreign languages used by missionaries to bring reading to the blind in their charge. The number of these was in the region of two hundred. Robert had been mainly instrumental in the translations of these, while William was full of thanksgiving that he had been able to bring so much of the Bible to so many.

Further horizons were yet to be met, and the influence of William's caring was to achieve even wider ones. He had been invited to Sweden and was impressed by the attitude of that country to their blind and other handicapped people. He returned home with a yet greater sense of gratitude than before.

Life at home progressed with as much calm as could be achieved. William found himself happier with Annie than he felt he had any right to expect. He had loved his first wife dearly, and now, of course, he also loved Annie. She had settled in with the family with the greatest ease, and with her charm and devotion to them all that was very comforting. William never ceased to give thanks to God every night in his prayers, for the joys that his life brought him.

The next major event was to be his visit to America. He had been asked if he would be willing to take his method over there, and, of course, he was delighted. Plans were made and eventually William and his daughter set off together for the great adventure.

At about this time a general appeal was launched for support for the care of the blind.

It must be remembered that early in the nineteenth century the blind were regarded as a nuisance. There was no provision for them of any kind at all in a general way. Any who were born, or became blind, who were fortunate enough to belong to a caring, more wealthy family, were treated kindly but for the hundreds, even thousands, of blind who came from poorer families, were left to their own devices.

William Moon remembered visiting a poor blind girl in London. He spoke to the child's mother, who took him upstairs to a poorly furnished room where two young girls lay in bed together. One had scarlet fever, and this brought back to William very vividly the cause of his own blindness. The other child was blind.

'What is she doing here?' asked William. 'Are you not afraid that she will get the disease herself?'

'There's nowhere else to put her, sir,' replied the woman. 'I can't have her wandering about downstairs when I'm busy, or out working. She might come to some harm. This is the safest place to put her.'

William was appalled. He took it upon himself to begin to teach the blind girl and was soon delighted at the change in her appearance. She was a quick learner. Not only did she soon begin to read, but eventually she was taught music, and came to be the organist at her church.

It was events such as this which caused William to suffer great heartache and when, after he had taught them, or had them taught by a helper, he saw the effects of this transformation in their existences, he praised God with a full heart.

So the appeal for help for these poor unfortunate disabled people, many of them mere children, was launched with vigour, and it was due to this that the general public came to appreciate the extent of the tragic situation. Money was freely subscribed. Not only that, but more helpers came forward and William began to feel that matters were improving. His thankfulness knew no bounds but, as ever in his serene and self-effacing way he exclaimed 'To God be the glory.'

The extent of William's work for the blind was beginning to be further appreciated in his own country. Missionaries working in many foreign lands had reason to be more than grateful to him for making it possible to bring reading to so many of their illiterate blind. Books, portions of the Scriptures and other helpful and informative items had been in the hands of people as far away as China. It was being brought home to the English people what a great pioneer he was. Home Teaching groups were growing, and it was William who had set them in hand. He was effortless in his activities, and as the work grew, so did his thankfulness to God, who, as William often said, had put this work in his hands. On occasion he was almost thankful that he had been prevented from becoming a minister of religion. He taught, spoke at meetings, and lived a life of service to others which was unsurpassed.

At about this time the USA began to show interest in this great work of bringing sight to the blind. It was not to be long before William was to make a tour over there, and so bring the benefits of his invention to hundreds more needy blind.

Queen Victoria herself was pleased to announce her support for, and admiration of the work being done, and this gave the Moon family much encouragement.

The family team was about to be deprived of Robert's valuable help, for he went over to America to become the Secretary of the Pennsylvania Home Teaching Society. Robert had always been his father's right hand man, and was certainly determined to follow in his father's footsteps.

Sir Charles Lowther, William's great friend, was to be a benefactor to those places in the USA which now had libraries for the blind. He donated a couple of thousand volumes for this purpose. William was more than grateful.

In the meantime work went on at home. William spoke at many meetings as well as supervising the embossing of many more books. His wife was invaluable in the way she ran the home as well as helping in the workshop whenever she could. Adelaide was kept extremely busy and found little time for outside interests. Indeed, the Moon team was still effective, and the great work went from strength to strength.

It was decided that the whole undertaking should now be put in the hands of trustees. William had always been meticulous in his dealing, and now felt that the time was ripe for a foundation to be laid for the mutual benefit of all concerned. The trustees included Sir Charles Lowther, The Rt. Hon. James Lowther, Lord Mount Temple, together with William and his daughter. This was a most satisfactory move, and William felt that the work could not be in better hands.

After some discussion with his wife and daughter at about this time, it was decided that William should be free to accept the invitations of the people in the USA, and go over there to give his support and to open up new ventures there. He set off with his daughter, leaving his wife to take charge of things at home with the help of the trustees and his faithful workpeople.

The great day arrived and William and Adelaide took the train at the start of their journey. Annie could only go as far as their local station to speed the departing ones, and she went slowly back home feeling a little bereft. Nevertheless, she was determined to carry on during their absence in the same way that they had done for so long now. Prayer was always the answer for them all, when help was felt to be needed.

William was always excited now, when he had occasion to go to London, and often wished he could see the glories of the new Victoria Station which had only been built in fairly recent times. Arriving there, he and Adele took a hansom to carry them to the station for the train to Liverpool, from which port their ship was due to sail.

Although a woman now approaching her forties, Adelaide was as excited as her father at the prospect of so long a journey; the sailing time would be about three weeks, and it seemed a rather wearisome wait until they could land on the other side.

But of course, land they did, and Adelaide then felt that she could use several sets of eyes to take in all the varied sights in order to describe them to her father.

William was reminded of the times when Robert and he had travelled to the Continent and Robert had been so valuable in describing what he saw to his blind father.

Wherever they went, people were delighted to be able to welcome them, and to see for themselves this great man who was still working every day for the benefit of those less fortunate blind. It was a great day when William was honoured in Pennsylvania by being awarded the honorary degree of Doctor of Laws. The American people were fully aware of all that William had achieved, and were most susceptible to his charm and kindness. Many of the blind people who met him were anxious to take his hand and thank him. It was a rewarding experience.

Back in England some months later, William felt he could never find enough time to tell Annie all about their adventures. She enjoyed all his stories, and, in turn, was able to tell him that in his absence the work had continued and had grown even further. William, of course, always concluded by giving thanks to God.

Chapter 11

TWO SOURCES OF GREAT SATISFACTION arose at about this time, but, in his usual modest way, William reminded everyone that any glory was God's and not his. The first was the fact that the government of the USA decided to free all imports of books for the blind from any duty. This was a great step forward, since William had established several teaching societies there, and books were constantly being exported from his works for their use.

The other source was a very unexpected gift of a couple of thousand pounds, given as a gift to enable William's premises to be enlarged, and thus to provide a greater scope for the production of his books.

Added to this was the fact that his sister had decided to return to England to make her home near him. William felt that his cup could not be more full.

At about this time a royal commission was set up to examine the state of the blind in England. The commission sent visitors to William's workshop, and took a great deal of evidence. This again, made William thankful that at last public opinion was being made aware of the deplorable state of the blind in general.

There was now another event of great import in the life of William and his family. William had been working for the benefit of the blind people for fifty years. Not a moment had ever been wasted. Day after day, sometimes to the extent of excessive exhaustion, he had brought his energies to the great self-imposed task. There was a celebration during which William was presented with various gifts which included a splendid clock, an illuminated address, a purse of money and many letters of congratulation. His work had been acknowledged throughout the world, and Australia had sent a book of names of blind people who had been given the power to read by means of William's invention. It was stated in one of the newspapers that William looked younger than ever and that his cheerful spirit permeated to the whole neighbourhood. William's only answer to all the praise was to say that God deserved all the glory, not he. One newspaper had printed an article during this time reminding people that the names of inventors of war machines were known widely, but that there were yet many who would be unable to put a name to this pioneer who brought sight to thousands of blind.

Annie and Adelaide were very proud of William and felt that it was only right and proper that he should receive thanks for all that he had done, and of course, still did. His work never lapsed.

This great pioneer, who had so selflessly given all that he had, and more, was greatly beloved. It was therefore a sad blow to many when it was learned that he had suffered a stroke. Fortunately this was a slight one, after which, with the assistance of an attendant who helped him about, he continued with his Sunday talks to the appreciative audiences who had followed his words for so many years. He had had to curtail some of his activities in the workshop, doing less than he had been used to do. This was of concern to him, so he still did as much as he possibly could.

It was October in the year eighteen hundred and ninety four. The weather was open and the winds were finally stripping the trees of their leaves. The Sunday dawned bright and clear and in the afternoon William, helped by his attendant, went to the Town Hall and spoke to those whom he had come to call 'his' people. His theme that day was, as it had been so often before, Thankfulness. It was the word by which he had lived ever since his blindness struck him over fifty years ago. His message came through loud and clear and he felt that his listeners went away with a feeling of satisfaction and hope.

A couple of days later William's attendant took him for a short walk. The sun was shining and, as William said, he could feel the warmth and felt comforted by it. They had been walking only a few minutes when William remarked that he was not feeling too well.

'Perhaps we had better turn back, Mr Moon,' said the helper. William agreed and they returned home.

Annie and Adelaide were in the sitting room when William was brought in. The attendant beckoned Annie aside and took her into the hall.

'I fear that your husband is not at all well. It is most unlike him to complain of any feeling of illness. I think he should perhaps go to bed and rest.'

Annie agreed to this and made a mental note to ask the doctor to call in next morning. She helped William into his bed and left the room.

Downstairs Adelaide had spoken again to the attendant, and they had decided that they would suggest to Annie that the doctor be called that day. Annie agreed to this, and the attendant went off to take the message.

The present doctor was one Doctor Evans, who had become William's good friend since he had taken over the practice. He examined William thoroughly and said that he thought it would be advisable for him to have a day or two in bed, with complete rest. This was agreed to, and Doctor Evans went away.

During that night William slept very little, and by the morning it was apparent that he was far from well. Doctor Evans was again summoned although he had promised to visit them again in two days' time.

William was evidently failing. He was very quiet, and although Annie took him something hot to drink, it was not touched. During the afternoon it was noticeable that William appeared to be failing. He did not complain, but lay still, now and then putting out his hand to take that of Annie or Adelaide. His sister had been told, and she came to the house before the afternoon had turned to evening.

It was then that William seemed to become more aware of the people around him. He smiled, and holding out his hand to Adelaide he grasped her own. He spoke quietly.

'Ever my inspiration and help, Adele.'

He had not used the pet name for her for a number of years. She felt tears spring to her eyes. She squeezed her father's hand and, bending to kiss him, said, 'Dearest Papa.'

William then heaved a great sigh. He spoke again.

'My life has been dark: it has been a dark night, but it has also been a bright day.'

He paused for breath, then continued.

'I have been greatly blessed. God gave me the talent of blindness, and I have done what I could with it.'

Saying these words, he sank back into his pillows and closed his eyes. It was finished. This great, selfless, spirit was free of whatever his blindness had cost him in silent suffering.

Early the next week William's funeral took place. Adelaide was reminded of that of her mother, when her father had stood before the congregation and spoke to them. She felt such a gap in her life now that she thought could never be filled.

The funeral took place in the cemetery outside the town. There were crowds of mourners, many of them blind, some of these carrying their embossed hymn books with them, in case of need. As the sound of the horses' muffled hooves approached, people turned towards the hearse, bowing their bared heads.

There were many tears shed that day, and many people went away with such a sense of loss that their teacher and friend was no longer with them.

So passed the man, pioneer in bringing sight to the blind, who had done more in this cause than any other person.

Epilogue

ALTHOUGH THIS BOOK HAS BEEN presented with imagination and the intimate life of William Moon written as fiction, the details of his wonderful pioneering work are true to life.

William Moon's invention is still available for the use of any whose reading sight has failed. Books of all kinds, together with many other publications may be obtained from the National Library for the Blind.

The author has every reason to be thankful to this great man, as she herself has lost her reading sight, and has found the literature available of great help.

Edna Stroud.